# The Creative Curriculum® for Family Child Care, 2nd Edition

## Volume 2: Routines and Experiences

Diane Trister Dodge, Sherrie Rudick,
and Laura J. Colker

TeachingStrategies™ • Washington D.C.

Editor: Laurie Taub
Design and layout: Abner Nieves
Illustrations: Anthony LeTourneau
Production: Judy Myers

Teaching Strategies, Inc.
P.O. Box 42243
Washington, DC 20015

www.TeachingStrategies.com
ISBN: Complete set: 978-1-60617-103-5
        Vol. 1: 978-1-60617-074-8
        Vol. 2: 978-1-60617-075-5

Teaching Strategies and The Creative Curriculum names and logos are registered trademarks of Teaching Strategies, Inc., Washington, D.C.


Library of Congress Cataloging-in-Publication Data

Dodge, Diane Trister.
  The creative curriculum for family child care / Diane Trister Dodge, Sherrie Rudick, and Laura J. Colker. -- 2nd ed.
      p. cm.
  Includes bibliographical references and index.
  ISBN 978-1-60617-074-8 (volume 1) -- ISBN 978-1-60617-075-5 (volume 2)  1.  Family day care--Activity programs--United States. 2.  Child development.  I. Rudick, Sherrie. II. Colker, Laura J. (Laura Jean) III. Title.
  HV854.D63 2009
  362.7'12--dc22
                                                                                2009016355


Printed and bound in the United States of America

2014    2013    2012    2011    2010    2009                    10   9   8   7   6   5   4   3   2   1

# Table of Contents

# PART II

# Routines

What do you think about when you hear the word *routines*? Do words like *boring, mechanical,* and *unexciting* come to mind? Although routines may not be exciting for adults, young children experience them very differently. For children, routines can be comforting, nurturing, and intimate, and they can be wonderful learning opportunities.

Routines are important times of the day for young children. Consistent and nurturing routines meet the physical and social–emotional needs of young children. They promote children's trust and autonomy, and they support other aspects of development and learning. The very fact that they are repetitive and predictable helps children form secure attachments with their caregivers.

Routines need to be managed in ways that enable you to focus your attention on the children and enjoy the time together. Here are some ways to make routines work well for you and the children:

- Follow recommended health and safety practices. This will help prevent the spread of diseases to you, your family, and the children in your care.
- Allow sufficient time during routines to meet individual needs without rushing.
- Talk about what you and the child are doing as you carry out the routine.
- Promote the development of self-care skills and children's increasing independence.
- Think of ways to involve school-age children in routines.
- Provide continuity between each child's home and the program. Use the "Family and Child Information Form" to learn how families carry out routines at home. Conduct routines in as many of the same ways as you can.
- Send home letters to families and *LearningGames* related to routines.

Each of the four chapters of part II focuses on one of the daily routines: hellos and good-byes, mealtimes, diapering and toileting, and sleeping and resting. Each chapter begins with some questions that encourage you to think about your views about a particular routine. Information about health and safety is included because routines require attention to those concerns. Each chapter describes setting up for the routine and explains how you can encourage development and learning during the routine. Finally, each chapter ends with a discussion of family partnerships because they enable you to provide consistent care for each child.

# Hellos and Good-Byes

# Hellos and Good-Byes

Families and children say hello to you and good-bye to one another as every day begins. Children reunite with their families and leave your home as every day ends. Children, their families, and you may experience strong feelings during these times. As you think about your practices, consider these questions:

**Do you say something unique and special to each child and family member every day when they arrive and depart?** How do you manage this when you are also caring for other children?

**What do you think about a child who cries a lot when his parents say good-bye?** What about a child who clings to you or one who is withdrawn and sad? How does a child's crying make you feel? Do you feel differently about a child who never cries at drop-off time?

**What might explain some parents' attempts to leave without saying good-bye?** What are they feeling? How do you feel when parents leave that way? How do the children feel? What can you do to help them realize that this is not in their children's best interest?

**How do you help family members reunite with their children at the end of the day?** How does a parent feel when her child has a temper tantrum or keeps playing? How do you feel?

Arrivals set the tone for the day. When morning farewells are painful, parents may suffer more than their children, who often recover quickly once they feel comfortable in your care. Once children learn that they can trust you and form a secure attachment with you, they are able to say good-bye to family members more easily.

Reunions at the end of the day can also be challenging. A child who said good-bye easily or who adjusted well after a painful good-bye might greet her father joyfully, but she might ignore him. She also might have a temper tantrum or begin to cry because she saved her strong feelings for her family, the people she trusts most. Departures often need your attention as much as arrivals.

Learning to separate from loved ones is an important part of growing up. When you help children manage separations from and reunions with their loved ones, they feel understood and gain self-confidence. Planning can make it easier for you to manage these times of the day.

# Setting Up for Hellos and Good-Byes

A well-organized setting and special items that connect children to their families can help ease arrivals and departures. Here are some suggestions:

**Include comfort items from home.** Familiar objects, such as a favorite blanket, stuffed animal, or special toy help young children feel more secure when they are away from those they love. Keep comfort items where children can find them.

**Display photos of children and their families.** Make an attractive wall display at the children's eye level. You can also fill a basket with family pictures so children can carry them around, or you might make a photo album or book of family pictures.

**Post a job chart.** A simple job, such as feeding a pet, watering plants, or setting out books in the living room, gives children an important responsibility.

**Have a sign-in system.** Signing their names or posting cards with their names and photos on a chart gives children a task to do as soon as they arrive. This eases the transition, and it is also a literacy activity.

**Display the daily schedule in pictures and words.** Learning the order of daily events often helps children feel more secure. You can show a child who asks, "When is Mommy coming?" exactly when that will happen. You can explain, "Let's look at the schedule. We're having snack now. Then we will go outside to play. When we come inside, you may play with toys. Then your mommy will be here!"

**Include quiet retreat places.** Sometimes children want to get away from the noise of a group and have some quiet time. This could be a comfortable chair, a cozy corner with large pillows, a loft, or a window seat.

**Display and read books about hellos and good-byes.** Books such as Becky Edwards' *My First Day at Nursery School* and Alice Low's *Mommy's Briefcase* can lead to discussions about separations and what parents do at work. Consider writing your own books with pictures of the children in your program.

**Include materials that encourage play about hellos and good-byes.** Offer opportunities for children to appear and disappear by playing in tunnels, cardboard boxes with doors that open and close, or tents made by draping a blanket over a table. Provide props such as hats, briefcases, tote bags, and empty food boxes to encourage twos and preschool children to pretend that they are leaving for work or going shopping and then coming home again. Provide toy phones so children can pretend to call their families.

# Caring and Teaching

Hellos and good-byes offer opportunities to build positive, trusting relationships with children and families. When you think about these routines as an important part of your curriculum, you can give children and their families the attention they need during these times.

## Easing the Transition

When a child first enters your program, you will need to allocate time and plan ways to ease the transition from family members' care to yours. Here are some suggestions:

**Arrange a transitional period with families.** Children need a little time to get to know you and to feel comfortable in this new setting while a family member is nearby. Help families understand the importance of this transitional period and encourage them to plan so they can take the time needed to ease their children into your program. However, you also need to recognize that job situations and other responsibilities may not allow family members to stay, even though they would like to do so.

**Spend extra time with each new child and family.** Show children where they will put their things, where the toys are, and where the various routines take place. As parents get to know you, they will feel more confident about leaving their children in your care. Children will feel more at ease when they see you spending time with their families.

**Be available when a child needs extra help.** Consider any special needs of the children in your program. A child with a disability may need extra time to adjust. A child whose home language is different from yours may be comforted by your speaking a few words or singing a simple song in his or her home language. A child who usually transitions easily may need extra comforting once in a while.

**Stay with an upset child and talk about feelings.** When a child has difficulty saying good-bye, it is tempting to rush through the process or to distract the child while a family member leaves. However, doing so will lead the child to distrust you and may make separation even more difficult. You want the child to learn that you understand how he feels and that you will help him deal with those feelings.

**Put out something interesting to do at arrival time.** Display a photo you took during a neighborhood walk or a new toy for families and children to explore together as children begin the day in your FCC home.

**Offer calming activities each day.** Playing musical instruments, dancing, squeezing dough, playing with sand or water, and hugging stuffed animals and dolls are examples of sensory activities that help children manage their feelings.

## Responding to What Children Need

Hellos and good-byes are wonderful opportunities to give each child individual attention when it is needed most. Children's ages and past experiences affect the ways they handle these times of the day. Knowing what to expect can help you respond appropriately.

**Infants** usually adjust well to new situations if their needs are met consistently and in a loving way. Before they are 6 months old, they have little difficulty separating from family members. This situation often changes around 8–10 months, when infants are more securely attached to their families and other special adults. A baby who never seemed to mind when left in your care might suddenly be upset when his parent says good-bye. While this is difficult for everyone involved, it is a good sign because it shows that the child has formed secure attachments to loved ones. Sometimes just a small change in a child's daily routine can make separating more difficult.

**Toddlers and twos** show great variability in being able to leave their parents. Some days they may run into your open arms at the door and cheerfully wave good-bye to their mother or father. On other days they may cling so tightly to their parents that you have to pull them off gently so that their parents can leave. If you have established positive relationships with children and they have a consistent routine in your program, then, even on the most challenging days, children will know that they can trust you to help them through difficult times.

The end of the day can be equally challenging for toddlers and twos. The same child who dissolved in tears when his mother left in the morning may have thoroughly enjoyed his day in your program and become completely involved in the routines and experiences you planned. When his mother comes to get him at the end of the day, he might seem hardly to notice. These situations have to be handled sensitively so the parent does not feel rejected.

**Preschool children** who are entering your program for the first time may have as much difficulty separating from their family members as an older infant, toddler, or 2-year-old. At this stage, children can talk about their feelings and learn to manage them. They understand the daily schedule and the fact that they return to their homes each day.

Sometimes events in a child's life can affect the way the child experiences separations. Lack of sleep, missing breakfast, or a parent who is away on a trip or deployed overseas for an extended time will cause a change in a child's behavior. You have to be prepared for situations to change at any time.

**School-age children** are generally able to handle arrivals and departures easily. They are still affected by your responses to their comings and goings. They want to know you are happy to see them when they are dropped off by their families or arrive from school. If you can give them a little one-on-one time during these transitions, you may find that they are more open with you about what is happening in their lives. They benefit immensely when you take time to connect with their families at the end of the day and say a good-bye to them cheerfully.

The ways you greet and say good-bye to children and their families enable you to develop trusting relationships and support learning. As you interact with children during the day, you help them develop a sense of competence that enables them to handle separations. Referring to curricular objectives can help you appreciate just how much children are learning.

| What You Might Do | Why |
| --- | --- |
| Hold a 2-year-old who is crying after his mother leaves. Reassure him, "You are very sad because your mommy left. You really want your mommy. She's going to work now. She'll come back to pick you up." | When you acknowledge a child's emotions and talk about what he is feeling, he learns that his feelings matter and you will help him manage them. *(Objective 1, Regulates own emotions and behaviors)* |
| Play peek-a-boo with an infant again and again. | Games that involve hiding and reappearing help a child learn that objects and (living) people exist even when they cannot be seen. The child also learns about imitating and pretending. *(Objective 12, Remembers and connects experiences)* |
| Follow consistent routines during the day. | Children feel more secure when they know what to expect. *(Objective 1, Regulates own emotions and behaviors)* |
| Explain to the mother of a preschool child who does not want stop playing that he is learning how to cope with transitions throughout the day. | You want to reassure the parent that this is normal behavior and does not mean that the child prefers staying in child care. Children often have trouble with changes and need time to cope with them. *(Objective 1, Regulates own emotions and behaviors)* |

| What You Might Do | Why |
| --- | --- |
| Talk with a preschool child who calls another child *baby* for crying when her mother leaves. Explain, "You get sad sometimes, too. She misses her mommy, but she'll feel better soon. Maybe you can find one of the toys you know she likes. Getting it for her might help her feel better." | You want to help the child become aware of and respect other people's feelings and learn how to respond in a positive manner. *(Objective 2, Establishes and sustains positive relationships)* |

## Partnering With Families

Take time to learn how each family handles arrivals and departures in other situations and what they think will help their child in your program. Here are some suggestions for working together:

**Respect individual differences.** Families have different ways of approaching separations and reunions. Some people value independence and think that very young children should be able to function separately from their families. Other people think that a mother should never be separated from her infant. As you work with families, try to get to know each family's beliefs so you can support them during hellos and good-byes.

**Learn about the special rituals families develop** and then use them each day. For example, you might hold an infant and say, "One kiss, two kisses. Bye-bye, Mommy," while her mother kisses her on both cheeks. Walk a toddler to the door to wave good-bye and blow kisses. Give a high-five to a preschooler who has just given one to his dad in their habitual farewell. Remind a school-age child to e-mail her mother when she arrives at your home after school. Rituals help children—and adults—feel more secure because they know what to expect.

**Suggest that families leave something personal with their children.** An object that belongs to a family member is a reminder to the child that his mother or father will come back. The parent might say to the child, "You are in charge of the book that we are reading together. Will you keep it with your things so we can find it when I pick you up?"

You can also make families your partners by using and sending home *LearningGames*® activities. Share the letter about hellos and good-byes when families first enroll in your program.

# LearningGames® for Hellos and Good-Byes

Birth–12 months

## Game 29, "Hi and Bye-Bye"

Share this *LearningGames* activity with families to help them understand that it is important to say simple words such as *hi* and *bye-bye*. Encourage them to notice any attempt the child makes to say them or similar words. As time goes by, point out the progress each child is making in this area.

12–24 months

## Game 46, "Hide-and-Seek"

When you share this game with the family, explain that something as simple as hiding and seeking is a step in the long process that helps children master separating and reuniting.

24–36 months

## Game 99, "Tell Family Stories"

Invite families to use stick puppets to tell stories about what family members do. Include some things that family members do during the day, such as going to work and coming home. Show them how you use stick puppets to involve children in storytelling and how you have the characters go away and return.

36–48 months

## Game 106, "Seeing Feelings"

Encourage families to play this game if their child feels sad when they leave in the morning or happy when they return in the afternoon. They can also play it if they notice another child expressing sad or happy feelings during hellos and good-byes. Explain how you help children interpret the emotional cues of others. For example, you might say, "Tamika looks sad. I think she feels sad because her mother just left to go to work. Let's see if we can make her feel better." Explain how pointing out and naming emotions helps children recognize what they are feeling and what others are feeling. Encourage children to help a child who feels unhappy.

48–60 months

## Game 179, "Mailing a Letter"

If appropriate, use the e-mail suggestion in the "Another idea" circle of this game to encourage a child to communicate with his family during the day. When you send the game home, explain the language and literacy benefits of writing and mailing a letter.

# A Letter to Families About Hellos and Good-Byes

Dear Families,

Every day, you and your child say good-bye to one another in the morning and hello again in the afternoon. These hellos and good-byes are children's first steps on a lifelong journey of learning how to separate from and reunite with important people in their lives.

Learning to say hello and good-bye to people we love is a process, not something to be achieved in the first week or month or even year of child care. Indeed, after many years of experience, we adults sometimes find it difficult to separate and reunite.

I make time for hellos and good-byes each day because they will always be an important part of your child's life. Being able to separate is necessary if children are going to develop as independent, competent people. Being able to reunite is necessary to building and maintaining caring, long-term relationships.

Here are some ways for us to work together:

- **Try to spend some time each morning and afternoon here with your child.** Your presence will help make the transition between home and child care easier for your child.

- **Never leave without saying good-bye.** It's tempting to want to leave quietly if your child is busy and not noticing you. By saying good-bye, you strengthen your child's trust in you. Your child can count on the fact you will not disappear without warning. When you are about to leave in the morning, I can help you and your child say good-bye.

- **Create good-bye rituals.** This may be as simple as walking to the door with your child, giving your child a giant hug before you leave, or waving good-bye near the living room window. Having a ritual offers you both the comfort of knowing what to do.

- **Bring familiar items from home.** I welcome family photos and other reminders of home that you want to share. Seeing these special objects will help your child feel connected to you throughout the day.

- **Make a special arrangement with your school-age child.** Children often want to connect with their families when they arrive after school. If you want a phone call or an e-mail message, we can make an arrangement.

By working together, we can help your child feel comfortable, secure, and confident about being in family child care.

Sincerely,

# Mealtimes

## 7

# Mealtimes

Are you a healthy eater? How does your approach to nutrition influence what and how you teach children about healthy eating?

What should mealtimes be like for the children in your family child care home? Should talking be encouraged? If so, who should talk? Should children be moving around or sitting down? Must children eat everything on their plates?

Have you ever used food as a reward or punishment? For example, have you ever given a child a cupcake for sitting still at lunch or not allowed a child to have a snack because he did not put his toys away? If so, what do you think the experience taught the child about food and eating?

Mealtimes and related activities such as setting the table, washing hands, talking with others at the table, and brushing teeth are a very important part of life in a family child care home. They are also wonderful learning opportunities for children. During these activities, you interact with children and help them get to know one another. You help them develop good nutrition and health habits. During mealtimes, children explore the tastes, colors, textures, and aromas of foods, and they enjoy a sense of caring and community.

Mealtimes in a family child care home also provide opportunities for children to be involved in preparing food. We talk more about this in chapter 18, "Cooking."

# Setting Up for Mealtimes

The kitchen, dining room, or a table in the play area may be the place for meals in a family child care home. Make children comfortable at the table. Pull infants' high chairs up to the table—and a chair for yourself—so you and the children can eat together.

Some family child care providers prepare meals for the children. Others ask families to bring their children's lunches each day. In either case, it is important to know about child nutrition and to follow sound health and safety practices.

Here are some important things to think about:

**Learn about good nutrition for children.** Serve healthy foods prepared in healthy ways. Avoid junk food snacks and empty calories. These contribute to childhood obesity, which is increasing. Talk to families about their children's favorite foods and incorporate familiar foods into your menus. The U.S. Department of Agriculture's (USDA) Child and Adult Care Food Program (CACFP) guidelines explain the requirements for breakfast, lunch, and snacks. (Related expenses are reimbursable if you are enrolled in the CACFP.) If you provide meals and have school-age children who come to your program before and after school, be sure to serve nutritious breakfasts and healthy snacks. Encourage children to drink water. The USDA Food and Nutrition Service has several excellent online resources that you may download. Look especially for the *Feeding Infants* publication and for the *Nibbles for Health* newsletters.

**Observe health and safety guidelines.** Kitchen counters are of a convenient height, so it is tempting to put an infant on the counter to change his or her diaper. However, to prevent the spread of disease, food-preparation and eating areas must always be separated from diapering and toileting areas as well as from laundry areas.

**Make handwashing a part of every meal- and snack time** for all children, even the youngest infants. Be sure to wash your own hands before you touch, prepare, or serve food. Rub soapy hands together for at least 10 seconds before rinsing with warm water. Dry your hands with a clean paper towel or a single-use cloth towel, and turn the taps with the towel. You may wish to put out a timer or teach children to sing a particular song to make sure that they spend enough time washing.

**Learn the rules for handling food safely.** There is a lot to know about safe food handling, preparation, and storage. Specific practices for safe food handling are too numerous to list here, but it is vital for you to know how to prevent foodborne illnesses. Young children are especially at risk for foodborne illnesses because their immune systems are not yet fully developed. Find out whether having a food handler's certificate is a licensing requirement in your state. Even if it is not, consider taking a food handler's course through your local adult education provider. There are several important sources of specific information about how to prepare, serve, and store food safely, whether it is made in your own kitchen or brought by families. These include 1) your state licensing standards; 2) *The National Association for Family Child Care Accreditation Standards Resource Manual: Health Standards for NAFCC Accreditation*; and 3) *Caring for Our Children: National Health and Safety Performance Standards: Guidelines for Out-of-Home Child Care Programs*, written by the American Academy of Pediatrics, American Public Health Association, and National Resource Center for Health and Safety in Child Care and Early Education.

**Childproof the kitchen.** Make sure that low cabinets have child safety locks and that all cleaning materials are stored out of children's reach in locked cabinets. If medicines are stored in the refrigerator, make sure they are also in a locked container. Set the water temperature no higher than 110 degrees Fahrenheit. The *Safety Standards for NAFCC Accreditation* include standards for kitchen safety and useful checklists to help you review your kitchen practices.

**Teach the children to be safe in the kitchen.** Teach the youngest children the meaning of *hot* to help them learn not to touch the stove. Be sure to turn your pot handles in and use the back burners when possible so children cannot pull pots off the stove and pour hot food on themselves.

**Have appropriate plates and utensils.** Use plates and eating utensils that are unbreakable, safe, and easy to handle. Toddlers and preschool children can learn to pour water, juice, and milk from small pitchers; to pass food; and to serve themselves from small plastic bowls. When pitchers and glasses are clear, children can see how much they have poured. Never use STYROFOAM™ materials or plastic utensils that can be broken easily. Have the food, utensils, and any equipment that you will need within an arm's reach so you can sit, eat, and converse with the children.

**Remember the special food-handling concerns for infants.** If you have infants in your family child care home, you need to know whether each baby is breast-feeding or drinking formula. If he or she is drinking formula, you need to know what kind of formula and how to prepare and store it. Breast milk must also be stored and warmed properly. Remember that you should never warm bottles or any other baby food in a microwave oven because the contents do not heat evenly. Instead, use a bottle warmer or crock pot (out of the children's reach), or warm the bottle under hot running water.

**Include a comfortable place for mothers who are breast-feeding.** The American Academy of Pediatrics says that breast milk is the best food for babies. They encourage mothers to breast-feed for at least a year. Assist breast-feeding mothers by providing a comfortable chair and, if requested, a private place. Include a pillow to support her baby on her lap, a footrest, and a glass of water to drink. Learn how to store expressed breast milk for times when the mother is unable to come.

**Never prop bottles.** Putting a baby to bed with a bottle of milk or juice can cause ear infections; choking; and baby bottle mouth, a severe form of tooth decay that may cause tooth loss.

**Learn techniques for comforting babies with colic.** About 10–15 percent of young infants in Western cultures develop colic, a condition that may last through the fourth month. Babies with colic tend to cry loudly, uncontrollably, and for a long time. They extend or pull their legs up to their stomachs; have enlarged stomachs; and pass gas. There is no apparent cause for colic, and most children outgrow the condition. Some experts recommend specific techniques, such as swaddling, that can help comfort a colicky baby.

**Be aware of and follow food precautions.** For example, do not give honey to infants under 12 months of age because their digestive systems are immature. Avoid giving infants under 12 months white table sugar, artificial sweeteners, corn syrup, egg whites, fried foods, shellfish, raw onions, and processed meats. Do not offer tomatoes and pineapple to infants before age 1. The high acidity of these foods can harm delicate mouth tissues.

**Avoid serving foods that might cause choking.** Children under age 3 should not eat certain foods because they are choking hazards. Hot dogs and peanuts are the most frequent causes of choking in children under age 3. Other foods on which children choke easily include raw carrots; raisins and similar dried fruit, such as cherries and cranberries; popcorn; whole grapes; blueberries; whole olives; corn; uncooked peas; nuts; peanut butter; crumbly cookies or crackers; jelly beans, and hard candy.

**Be aware of children's allergies.** Some common food allergies include chocolate, strawberries, peanut butter, other nuts, and tofu. Find out from families if a child is allergic to these or other foods. If there are other adults in your FCC home, make sure all are aware of this information. Post it in your kitchen as a reminder to everyone.

# Caring and Teaching

Remember that the attitudes that children develop about food and nutrition can have a lifelong impact. You can do many things to make mealtimes enjoyable and to foster positive attitudes about food and nutrition:

**Plan ahead.** Mealtimes can be a challenge in a family child care home, especially if you are providing children's meals. Make sure that children are engaged in easily supervised or self-directed activities while you are cooking. Keep meals simple but nutritious. When you make your family's dinner, consider making extra food for the children's lunch the next day. Alternatively, during the weekend you might cook and freeze food to serve during the week. Try to have everything ready when the children come to the table, including food, beverages, dishes, and utensils, so that you do not have to leave the table to get missing items.

**Feed infants when they are hungry.** Watch and listen for cues that babies are hungry and feed them as soon as possible. Before becoming so hungry that they cry, infants often show that they are ready to be fed by opening their mouths, making sucking sounds, and moving their hands randomly. You will be holding young infants in your arms while feeding them, so make sure that you have a comfortable glider or soft chair to sit in. Snuggle with the baby. Even when babies can hold the bottle by themselves, they still want to be held and enjoy your special time together.

**Create a calm and pleasant atmosphere.** A quiet activity, such as a story before lunch, helps to set a relaxed tone. Keep waiting times as short as possible and allow children enough time to eat. Sit and eat with the children. Talk together during mealtimes about familiar topics of interest to the children, such as the tastes and smells of the food you are eating, activities you did earlier in the day, or plans for the afternoon. Create an after-meal ritual, such as brushing teeth or looking at a book to get ready for nap time.

**Encourage children to help in whatever ways are appropriate for their levels of development.** Seat an infant on your lap so she can hear and watch the other children. Offer a mobile infant a chance to use his fingers to feed himself. Provide spoons that are easy to hold for toddlers who want to feed themselves. Invite 2-year-olds and preschool children to help set the table and do other mealtime tasks. Encourage school-age children to prepare snacks for the group. Many providers offer snacks at a self-serve table so children can help themselves when they are hungry.

**Make mealtimes social.** Sit with the children. Chat with them and encourage them to talk with each other about the events of the day. Mealtime conversations are opportunities for children to hear and practice using interesting, descriptive language as they "munch on crunchy green lettuce" or eat "lumpy, bumpy oatmeal."

**Make cleanup as easy as possible.** Toddlers, twos, preschool children, and school-age children can help clean up after meals and snacks if you provide child-sized equipment. Spills are inevitable, so be prepared. Place extra napkins and paper towels nearby where children can reach them, and invite them to help clean up spills.

**Recognize children's new skills and accomplishments.** Make a positive comment when you see a child learning to hold a bottle, drink from a cup, spread cottage cheese on a cracker, or cut a banana with a knife.

**Avoid struggling over food.** Encourage children to try new foods but do not force them. Talk about new foods, serve them in attractive ways, and taste everything, yourself. Allow children to control the quantity of food they eat. Do not expect them to eat everything on their plates.

**Never use food as a reward or punishment.** It is not all right to threaten to withhold food or to bribe a child to do something for an extra snack. This also means that you may not tell children that they have to eat their vegetables if they want to have dessert. Remember that a healthy dessert, such as fruit, is part of the meal, not a reward.

**Offer experiences that encourage children to practice mealtime skills throughout the day.** For example, include plates and eating utensils as props for dramatic play. Provide pitchers and small cups for water play, and encourage conversations throughout the day.

**Challenge school-age children to think about nutrition and foods from various cultures.** Involve them in planning menus. To encourage them to eat nutritious meals and snacks, have them look at the USDA's "MyPyramid for Kids" and other publications for children. Challenge them to read food labels and to evaluate food advertisements. Have them experiment with foods from different places. They can try eating with chopsticks or compare a homemade taco with a taco from a restaurant.

**Consider children's and family's preferences when developing your menus.** Include nutritious foods that are children's favorites and familiar foods that they eat at home.

**Consult with specialists about a child with a disability that affects eating.** They can advise you about feeding procedures as well as about appropriate adaptive equipment.

## Responding to What Children Need

Mealtimes are one of the best ways of putting the "family" in family child care. They are opportunities for nurturing, linking children's homes with your program, and promoting children's development and learning.

| What You Might Do | Why |
|---|---|
| Cradle a young infant in your arms while you feed him his bottle. Smile at him as he curls his fingers over yours and gazes into your eyes. | When you share this special time with a child, you give the message, "You can trust me to take care of you." *(Objective 2, Establishes and sustains positive relationships)* |
| Encourage toddlers to practice self-care tasks such as setting the table, eating with a spoon, pouring milk, and helping to clean up after lunch. | Preparing and eating meals and cleaning up afterward are wonderful opportunities for toddlers to become more independent and to gain confidence in their own abilities. *(Objective 7, Demonstrates fine motor strength and coordination)* |
| Serve potatoes in different ways (boiled potatoes one day, and mashed or baked the next). Talk about how potatoes change when you cook them and which types the children like best. | The simple potato can support vocabulary development, a math experience (charting the children's preferences), and a science experiment (raw potatoes are harder than boiled potatoes). *(Objective 9, Uses spoken language to express thoughts and needs; Objective 22, Compares and measures; Objective 26, Demonstrates knowledge of the physical properties of objects and materials)* |
| Involve school-age children in planning menus. Have them look at the USDA's "MyPyramid for Kids" and other publications for children to make sure that meals are nutritious. | This challenges them to do research and learn about nutrition. It also gives them practice in making decisions and a way to contribute to the program in a meaningful way. |

# Partnering With Families

Food plays an important role in family life. It is often influenced by cultural and family traditions. Mealtimes offer wonderful opportunities to strengthen partnerships with families.

Partnerships are especially important for the very young children in your family child care home. Food and feeding practices have to be carefully coordinated with families for health reasons. Here are some suggestions:

**Discuss special feeding issues with families** when their children enroll, especially with the families of children younger than age 3. Topics to discuss include nursing; weaning; introducing solid food; burping techniques; allergies; and, if families provide meals, what food to bring.

**Introduce new foods to babies after the family has introduced them** at home first. When you try a new food, allow time—usually 5 days—before introducing another. That way, if the child has an allergic reaction, you have a better chance of identifying which food is causing the problem.

**Talk with each family about what their child eats at home and in your program.** Share your menus. If families provide their children's lunches, suggest safe and nutritious foods. You may want to keep records of what and how much children eat during the day and send home brief notes with this information to help families plan their children's meals and snacks at home.

**Respect and follow families' preferences and special food requests as much as possible** within the Child and Adult Care Food Program requirements, whether for reasons of health, culture, religion, or personal preference. If differences arise, talk with the family about them. Families' viewpoints might be different from yours about such things as self-feeding, messiness at mealtimes, playing with food, and sitting at the table.

**Talk with families about how they celebrate birthdays and other holidays at home.** Think about how to balance good nutritional practices with celebrations. Develop a policy and share it with families. Decide whether you will ask families to bring food for birthdays and holidays or whether you will provide it, and whether you will you celebrate special days with cake and candy or with more nutritious foods.

**Invite mothers to come to the program to nurse their infants at any time.** Provide a comfortable place where they can be with their babies without interruption.

**Invite families to join their children for meals and snacks** whenever they can. Having family members present can help ease separation anxieties and help children make the connection between eating at their homes and eating at your family child care home.

Working with families helps build continuity between each child's home and the family child care home. This helps children feel comfortable and secure. The following *LearningGames®* activities and the letter to families are two other ways to communicate with families about mealtimes.

## *LearningGames®* for Mealtimes

### Birth–12 months

### Game 32, "Things to Taste"

Putting things in their mouths is one of the ways that babies use their senses to learn about the world. Sometimes they like what they taste, but sometimes they don't! Explain to families that in your family child care home you let babies choose what they want to eat, how much they want, and how long they want to explore the taste. This helps children develop positive attitudes toward eating, and it helps them learn to make choices.

### 12–24 months

### Game 56, "Expressing Needs"

Young children express their needs by using simple words and gestures. The more clearly children express their needs verbally, the more likely their needs will be met. While this game is geared for children from 12–24 months, babies express their needs through sounds and gestures, and preschool children are still learning to use words to communicate their needs. This game is easy to play at mealtimes. You model language, for example, "Do you need a spoon for your cereal? I'll get it for you."

### 24–36 months

### Game 96, "Help Him Help Himself"

This game is played at mealtimes. Encourage families to let children serve themselves and to make choices about the food they put on their plates, just as you let them choose. Show them the large spoons and small pitchers you use to promote family-style dining in your FCC home.

36–48 months

### Game 133, "Packing My Own Picnic"

A great weekend activity is to invite children to pack a picnic lunch all by themselves to eat in the backyard or the park. It doesn't matter if the experience doesn't go perfectly. Like all of us, children can learn from their mistakes. Maybe everything will go better next time. Look for a nice day to encourage children in your program to pack lunch and take it outside for a picnic.

---

48–60 months

### Game 157, "Fork Foods"

Fork, spoon, or fingers? Use this activity to help children practice a very important skill—classification—as they draw or paste pictures of food in the appropriate places on a chart (fork food, spoon food, or finger food). Show families the chart or poster you and the children make. Encourage families to make charts or posters at home and to share them with you.

# A Letter to Families About Mealtimes

Dear Families,

One of the best things about a family child care home is that we enjoy breakfast, lunch, and snacks together in much the same way as your family does. Our meal- and snack times are special. The children help set the table, we sit and eat together, and the children help clean up afterward. You might be surprised to see a 2-year-old carefully pouring milk into a cup from a small pitcher. You might also see our preschool children passing bowls of food and serving themselves, or helping to clean up spilled milk. While we eat, we chat about what we've done during the day and whether we like a food that the children are trying for the first time. The children often help prepare the healthy meals and snacks we eat, and they are proud of this accomplishment.

Mealtimes and related activities, such as setting the table, washing hands, talking with others at the table, and brushing teeth, are all learning opportunities. Snacks and meals give your child a chance to feel cared for and to develop self-care, communication, and social skills. Mealtimes also give children chances to begin practicing good manners and healthy habits.

Here are some ways for us to work together:

- **Please tell me about mealtimes in your home.** What does your child eat and drink? What are your child's favorite foods? What foods does your child dislike? Do you have special family foods? What do you talk about? If I know this, I can talk about family meals and serve some of the same food. This will help your child feel connected with you during the day.

- **Join us for a snack or meal whenever you can.** Your child will love having you with us. So will I. In addition, you will have a chance to see how we do things, to ask questions, and to make suggestions. Of course, if you are nursing your child, please come at any time. I have a comfortable place where you can feed your baby without interruption.

- **Let's communicate about changes in your child's diet or eating habits.** For example, please let me know when your pediatrician recommends adding new foods for your baby. After you introduce a food at home, I'll introduce it here. We can also work together when your baby is weaned from the bottle. Let me know if your toddler's appetite is changing, or if your preschool or school-age child is refusing to eat a food he or she used to like.

- **Give me any information I need to keep your child healthy.** For example, let me know if your child has food allergies or a tendency to gag or choke. Please keep me informed of any changes.

Together, we can make mealtimes enjoyable and valuable learning experiences for your child.

Sincerely,

# Diapering and Toileting

**8**

# Diapering and Toileting

How do you feel when you are changing diapers? How do your feelings about soiled diapers influence your interactions with children during this routine?

How do you react when a child has a toileting accident? What do you say and do? What messages do you want children to receive?

What do you want to teach children about their bodies during diapering and toileting? Are you comfortable with talking about body parts? How do you react when children find humor in toileting?

Before you were a family child care provider, did you ever think that the bathroom would become one of the hubs of your home? Whether you are changing a baby's diaper, helping a 2-year-old learn to use the toilet, or reminding a preschool child to wash her hands every time she uses the toilet, diapering and toileting are a core routine in family child care.

Diapering and toileting might not be your favorite daily routine, especially if you concentrate on the messy and smelly aspects, but try to think of it positively. When you approach diapering and toileting as opportunities for meaningful interactions, rather than as tasks to hurry through, children learn important lessons. You teach them that bodily functions are a normal, healthy part of everyday life; that they can do many things for themselves; that they can take good care of themselves and stay well by always remembering to wash their hands after toileting.

# Setting Up for Diapering and Toileting

There are two important things to think about as you set up for diapering and toileting. First, make sure the area is inviting and attractive so you and the children will enjoy spending time there. Second, make it as convenient as possible. Diapering and toileting go smoothly and safely when the area is well-arranged and has room for storage.

## The Diapering Area

Here are important considerations for your diapering area:

**Find the best type of diaper-changing table and identify a good place for it.** Diaper tables come in different heights. Choose one carefully! Prevent back injury by finding one that is a good height for you, taking into account that you will have to lift the baby up and over a 6-inch railing. You can also save wear and tear on your back if you have a sturdy step stool so toddlers and twos can climb up to the table rather than have you lift them. Toddlers and twos love climbing, so this arrangement makes everyone happy.

If your bathroom is large enough, it is the ideal place for a sturdy diaper-changing table. If not, you'll have to find another spot for it. It is best located close to a handwashing sink. In fact, the American Academy of Pediatrics specifies that the changing table must be within 10 feet of a handwashing sink and preferably right next to the sink.[1] Are you looking for a convenient place to put it? The Academy also suggests that, if all else fails, the diaper table may be placed in the bathtub. If the whole table does not fit, try putting just two of the table legs in the tub. To avoid contamination, the changing table also *must* be away from food-preparation areas. The kitchen sink should not be used as the sink for diapering and toileting. Furthermore, the changing table should be used only for diapering. This is sometimes difficult because it can be a convenient place to put things down, but resist the temptation!

Babies can also be changed on the floor, rather than on a changing table. Some mobile infants, toddlers, and two-year-olds prefer to stand while being changed. Whatever you do, though, make sure that the surface is washable and can be sanitized after each use. Avoid changing children on beds, sofas, or other furniture that cannot be washed and sanitized easily. Of course, don't use the kitchen floor!

**Keep all of your supplies within reach:** diapers, wipes, gloves, and bleach solution. Once the baby is on the table, you may not leave to get clean clothes or any other supplies. You must *never* leave a baby alone on a changing table, not even for a second. Although the table may have straps and guardrails, you cannot rely on them to keep the baby safe. Also remember that you can only reach for supplies with one hand because you must always keep the other hand on the baby.

**Make fresh bleach solution every day** and **keep a practical diaper can nearby.** Keep the solution close at hand but out of the reach of all children. You will need to have it handy so you can wash, rinse, and sanitize the diaper table after each diaper change. A step-on, foot-pedaled, or other type of hands-free diaper can will also help keep the diapering area sanitary.

If school-age children are in your care, remember that, unlike younger children who often like to share the toileting experience with their friends, school-age children need privacy. With rare exceptions, they can handle toileting on their own and remember to wash their hands without constant reminders.

## The Bathroom

Here are important considerations for your bathroom:

**Consider the best set-up for children who are learning to use the toilet.** The American Academy of Pediatrics and the American Public Health Association recommend using modified toilet seats and step aids for toilet learning. They discourage potty chairs because they are difficult to clean and sanitize.[2] If you use potty chairs, be sure to follow the guidance on cleaning and sanitizing them.

**Make it as easy as possible for children to use the toilet independently.** Arrange the environment so children can be successful and feel competent. Think about how you can make it easy for children to use the toilet and sink. Some children feel more comfortable with a modified toilet seat, and some need a sturdy step stool to reach the toilet. Most need a stool to reach the sink. Put soap and paper towels where children can reach them. If you post the steps of handwashing at their eye level, children can follow them independently. They will also strengthen their literacy skills at the same time!

**Make the bathroom pleasant and attractive.** Add special touches, such as a full-length, shatterproof mirror as well as a mirror over the sink. Display photographs of a child washing her hands, a child brushing his teeth, and a child tossing a paper towel in the trash can.

**Adapt the area as necessary for children with disabilities.** Many different toilet seats are designed to meet the needs of children with various disabilities. Families and therapists can advise you about appropriate equipment, such as handrails to make it easy to transfer between a wheelchair and the toilet.

# Caring and Teaching

If a child's diaper is changed six times a day until he is 30 months old, he will have had his diaper changed more than 5,400 times. Anything a child experiences 5,400 times is an important part of life for him and for you. As they experience this routine with you, children can tell how you feel about diapering and toileting by your tone of voice, body tension, and facial expression. Because you are important to the children in your care, it is important to view diapering and toileting positively.

## Keeping Children Safe and Healthy

One of your most important responsibilities as a family child care provider is to keep children safe and healthy. Diapering involves germs that may spread if you are not careful. Stools sometimes carry germs that can cause illnesses with diarrhea and vomiting, as well as serious diseases such as hepatitis A. For this reason, procedures for diaper changing and handwashing must be followed carefully. Follow these guidelines to make diapering and toileting as safe and healthy as possible:

> **Follow recommended procedures for changing diapers.** This routine, which is, repeated a dozen times a day in your family child care home, is more complex than you might think! *Caring for Our Children: National Health and Safety Performance Standards: Guidelines for Out-of-Home Child Care Programs* outlines eight steps for diapering, from organizing supplies to handwashing. Do you know, for instance, that washing the child's hands is part of diapering and that, if you wear gloves, there is a particular way to remove them? Do you know that to clean the diaper table you must wash it with detergent and water, rinse it with water, sanitize it with a surface bleach solution, and let it air dry? (Use 1/4 cup of liquid chlorine bleach to 1 gallon of water or 1 tablespoon of liquid chlorine bleach to 1 quart of water. Make the bleach solution each day, be sure to label the bottle, and keep it out of the children's reach.)

> **Schedule regular times to check children's diapers and change diapers between times as needed.** The American Academy of Pediatrics and American Public Health Association recommend that diapers be checked at least hourly for wetness and feces.[3]

> **Remain aware of the other children while diapering a child or taking a child to the bathroom.** Watch, listen, and use your good sense to recognize when you are needed by other children.

## Responding to What Children Need

Depending on their developmental levels and personal characteristics, different children react to diapering and toileting very differently. As during all daily routines, what you say and do make a difference in how children feel about themselves. The nice thing about diapering and toileting (yes, there really is a nice aspect!) is that you focus on an individual child. Make diapering and toileting special. Sing together and play games such as "Where Are Your Toes?".

Handle children's bodies respectfully. When you change a diaper, or help a toddler or preschool child use the toilet, consider how you handle her body. Do you lift her swiftly into the air and then quickly lay her down on the changing table? Do you stop, bend to her, smile, tell her that you are going to pick her up, let her know that you need her help, and then pause and wait for her reaction before gently lifting her up? By interacting gently throughout the diapering and dressing process, you let children know that you respect their bodies. When lifting young infants, remember to support their heads and necks.

Encourage children to participate in any way they can and talk with them about what you are doing. Use caring words and a calm voice during diapering and toileting. Describe what you are doing as you do it: "Here's your dry shirt. I will put your head through this part…Your arm goes in here…There it is! Your clean shirt is also right on your tummy!" Learn and use words in children's home languages for body parts and articles of clothing.

**Infants** interact with you individually during diapering. They also begin exploring and learning about their bodies and things around them. They vocalize in back-and-forth exchanges, pausing to listen as you converse. As they get older, they begin to participate more in the diapering routine. They lift their legs so you can take off the diaper, hold their hands out to be washed, tug on wet pants, and bring you a diaper. They begin to learn new words, such as words for body parts and clothes and words for concepts such as up–down, wet–dry, open–close, and cool–warm.

**Toddlers and twos** are becoming very interested in their bodies and bodily functions. They are able to participate more actively in diapering. They can get their own diapers from their cubbies, pull down their own pants, and often try to take off their wet diapers. Two-year-olds are about to learn something important—how to use the toilet— and you have an important role to play. If you and the child's family follow the child's lead, are supportive, work together, and avoid power struggles, you can help make toilet learning a pleasant experience. Here are some of the ways that children show that they are becoming more aware of their bodily functions and that they are or will soon be ready for toilet learning:

- staying dry for long periods of time
- wanting to sit on the toilet with their clothes on
- telling you that they are wet, had a bowel movement, or are going to (although they usually tell you too late to get them to the bathroom in time)
- saying that they want to use the toilet and talking about their urine and bowel movements, using whatever words are used at home

To help a child learn to use the toilet, follow these steps:

**Watch for signs that the child is ready.** Remember that 2-year-olds do not automatically become ready on their second birthday. While some twos show signs of readiness, many children are not ready to undertake this big step until they are at least 30 months old.

**Encourage children to use the toilet when they seem ready.** Talk with them consistently and calmly, but without undue pressure or shaming them.

**Frequently remind children to go to the toilet.** That way, they might not get so involved in what they are doing that they forget and have an accident. Make young children's toileting a social activity so they can see and learn from one another.

**Acknowledge children's successes.**

**Allow children to see their urine and bowel movements and invite them to help flush them if they choose.** Children react to flushing in different ways. Some are frightened; others want to flush again and again.

**Treat toileting accidents matter of factly.** Expect twos to have toileting accidents as they learn to control when and where they go to the bathroom. If you handle toileting accidents calmly, children will develop positive attitudes about using the toilet.

**Preschool children** can be fairly independent in the bathroom if it is set up so they can reach the toilet, sink, soap, paper towels, and trash can. They may still need help wiping themselves. They may enjoy making faces in front of the mirror with their friends or think of the sink as a great place for water play. Toileting is a social routine for some preschool children, but others prefer privacy. They are quite aware of differences in bathroom behavior for boys and girls. Keep in mind that preschool children may still have an occasional toileting accident. Because they are older, they may be more embarrassed than a 2-year-old who has a toileting accident, so it is important to react positively and calmly.

**School-age children** need little assistance, if any, with toileting and handwashing. Because children may have restrictions on when they may use the toilet at school, they might need a reminder to go to bathroom when they first arrive at family child care. Young school-age children may be quite curious about the physical differences between boys and girls. They may also take delight (as do twos and preschool children) in prohibited language, including bathroom language and language about body parts. You can encourage thoughtful bathroom behavior for boys by reminding them to put the toilet seat down.

| What You Might Do | Why |
| --- | --- |
| Take your time as you interact with each child during diapering, rather than rushing through the routine as quickly as possible. | You interact with children individually during diapering and toileting, and your responsive care helps build secure attachments. *(Objective 2, Establishes and sustains positive relationships with adults)* |

| What You Might Do | Why |
|---|---|
| Explain to the baby, "I'm going to pick you up and take you to the changing table. We'll get you some nice clean diapers." | Talking about what you are doing shows respect and helps children develop positive feelings about their bodies. *(Objective 1, Regulates own emotions and behaviors; Objective 13, Listens and understands increasingly complex language)* |
| Read books such as *Everybody Poops* with children who are learning to use the toilet. | Elimination of waste is a natural bodily function, and young children are curious about it. Reading a book about toileting can support a child who is struggling with this new developmental task. *(Objective 12, Performs self-care tasks; Objective 31, Comprehends and responds to books and other texts)* |
| Post pictures of the steps of handwashing above the sink in the bathroom. | Support children's independence by making it easy for them to follow the steps. Post them in order from left to right, to promote awareness of print conventions. *(Objective 30, Demonstrates knowledge of print and its use)* |
| React calmly to bathroom humor and toileting language, but let children know that it is unacceptable. | Bathroom humor and talk are typical, especially of toddlers and young school-age children. Overreacting may encourage such behavior and language, rather than discourage them. *(Objective 1, Regulates own emotions and behaviors; Objective 6, Follows limits and expectations)* |
| Use conventional terms for body parts, but accept children's use of other terms. | This gives the message that you are comfortable with these words and that body parts and elimination are not shameful. *(Objective 43, Demonstrates knowledge about self; Objective 18, Uses an expanding vocabulary)* |

# Partnering With Families

Family members and you are likely to have strong feelings and ideas about diapering and toileting, and theirs may be different from yours. Diapering and toileting are intimate and very closely related to people's feelings about their bodies. Especially if they do not know what words to use, families may be uncomfortable with talking about this routine. They might be ashamed when a child has a toileting accident or wets a bed in your FCC home.

You may have differences with families about strategies for toilet learning. Some families think that teaching a child to use the toilet means that the adult should take responsibility for getting the child to the bathroom at the right time. With this in mind, they may begin toileting learning when children are as young as 6 months. Others think that learning to use the toilet should begin when a child is ready to assume responsibility, him- or herself, typically around 30 months of age.

Here are some strategies to help you work with families on diapering and toileting:

**Find out how each family handles diapering at home.** When a child in diapers enters your program, ask about the kind of diapers the family uses, how often the child's diaper is changed at home, times that the child usually needs a diaper change, and any special instructions for diapering. Be clear about whether you or the family will provide diapers and how you will communicate if a family needs to replenish the supply. The "Family and Child Information Form" in the appendix of volume 1 includes some questions about how families handle this routine at home.

**Ask parents how they are helping their child learn to use the toilet at home.** Listen carefully and try to understand families' perspectives when they do things differently from you. Discuss the signs that a child is ready for toilet learning. Describe your approach. Negotiate differences if necessary. Things do not have to be done exactly the same at home as in family child care, but children need to know what to expect.

**Offer resources to families who are concerned about toileting.** Display books and articles. Encourage families to share their experiences with each other. Know when to suggest that a family talk to a doctor about a concern. The *LearningGames®* activities described below and the letter to families about diapering and toileting can help you coordinate this routine with families.

## *LearningGames®*

### Birth–12 months

### Game 14, "Show Feelings"

Families will enjoy playing this *LearningGames* activity as they lift their babies on and off the diaper table. This game helps families make diaper changing into a special, exciting, fun time, just as you do in your program. Babies look forward to having their diapers changed as they begin to anticipate what happens when their parents say, "Up you go!" and "Down you come!" This game helps babies learn about happy feelings, and the activity also encourages language development. It is a good activity to repeat during any of the routines.

12–24 months

## Game 49, "Sing Together"

"This is the way we change your diaper, change your diaper, change your diaper. This is the way we change your diaper, early in the morning." Add verses for "wash our hands… put on our coats…go to school..," and families have a fun game to play throughout the day. Encourage families to make up songs using their children's names, to pass on traditional family songs, and to sing in other languages.

24–36 months

## Game 72, "Me in a Mirror"

Watching himself in a mirror helps a child connect what he sees with what he feels his body doing. The bathroom is a great place for children to smile, make faces, brush teeth, wash faces, and, in general, see how they look in a mirror. Encourage families to describe children's actions (for example, "You're washing your nose") or tell what children are wearing (for example, "You're wearing your favorite striped shirt").

36–48 months

## Game 118, "Button and Zip"

Bathroom routines include opportunities for adults to help children practice zipping, buttoning, and snapping as they fasten their pants. If those tasks are difficult at first, families can help children build fine motor skills by practicing with the large buttons and buttonholes on sweaters and by helping family members zip their coats.

48–60 months

## Game 184, "I'd Like Help"

Knowing when and knowing how to ask for help are important, especially as tasks become more difficult. Encourage families to choose a phrase for their children to use when they need help, such as "I need your help with…," or "Will you please help me…?" Children can practice using the phrase during toileting and other times of the day, and even by asking for help during pretend play.

[1] American Academy of Pediatrics & American Public Health Association. (2002). *Caring for our children: National health and safety performance standards: Guidelines for out-of-home child care programs. A joint collaborative project of American Academy of Pediatrics, American Public Health Association,* and *National Resource Center for Health and Safety in Child Care* (2nd ed.). Elk Grove Village, IL: The Academy and Washington, DC: American Public Health Association. Also available at http://nrckids.org.

[2] Ibid.

[3] Ibid.

# A Letter to Families About Diapering and Toileting

Dear Families,

Diapering and toileting are daily events in a family child care home. I change babies' diapers, help children learn to use the toilet when they are ready, and help children develop good health habits such as washing their hands after toileting.

Although diapering may not be your favorite task, it can be a special time for you and your child. It offers a chance to focus all of your attention on your child. You can talk together, sing, or play a game of "Where Are Your Toes?". When you approach diapering as an opportunity to spend time with your baby, rather than as an unpleasant task to hurry through, you teach your child an important lesson: that bodily functions are a normal, healthy part of everyday life.

Over time, your child will become physically, cognitively, and emotionally ready to begin using the toilet. We will work together to make this a good experience for your child, and we will celebrate this milestone together.

Here's how we can work together:

- **Let's share information about diapering and toileting.** Tell me how you approach diapering at home. How often do you change your baby's diaper? How do you know that the diaper needs to be changed? What kind of diapers do you use? Are there any special instructions for diaper changes? Let me know what words your child will use to tell me that he or she needs to use the toilet.

- **We can talk about how to work together to help your child learn to use the toilet.** We'll look together for signs that your child is ready. We'll also talk regularly about your child's progress. Then we can decide together about ways to support your child and resolve any differences we may have.

- **Remember that toileting accidents are normal.** Learning to use the toilet takes time. Even children who can use the toilet successfully sometimes have toileting accidents. We can both respond to these in a matter-of-fact way.

- **Please make sure I have diapers and changes of clothing.** Don't be surprised if I send home soiled clothing in a tightly closed plastic bag. Germs can be spread easily during diaper changing, and experts tell us not to rinse soiled clothing in family child care homes. This procedure helps to keep your child healthy.

By keeping a sense of humor, we can make diapering and toileting times enjoyable and a time for learning.

Sincerely,

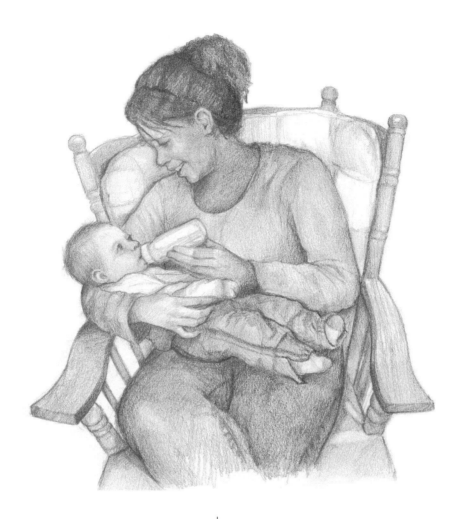

# Sleeping and Resting

# Sleeping and Resting

Can you think of a bedtime ritual that helped your own children or other children in your care? What was it? How did it make the child feel about going to sleep?

How do you help a young child relax enough to go to sleep? How do you help children transition from sleeping to being awake?

Why might a child cry or have difficulty falling asleep? Do you let children sleep until they wake up by themselves, or do you wake them at certain times?

What do you do about children who do not take a nap or who wake up early? What provisions do you make for those children?

What will you do if a family asks you not to have a child sleep or rest? How do you resolve differences with families?

Sleep and other forms of rest are necessary for healthy growth and development, so they are important parts of a program for young children. Very young infants sleep most of the day, waking only for diapering, feeding, and other care. Active toddlers and 2-year-olds spend more time awake than asleep, but they nap for an hour or more to restore themselves. They sometimes take both a morning and afternoon nap. Most preschool children still need a daily nap, usually after lunch. Even children who do not want to sleep benefit from a rest time away from group activities. When school-age children arrive at the end of the day, they also benefit from a quiet time to relax and restore themselves before starting their homework.

# Setting Up for Sleeping and Resting

Sleeping places in your family child care home will depend on whether you have a separate or shared space for your program. If you share space, children may sleep or rest in your family's bedrooms and beds, with clean bedding, of course. If they sleep in a space dedicated to family child care, you will need cribs, cots, or mats that are appropriate for the ages of the children in your group.

Many children prefer a cool, quiet, dimly lit place to sleep. If some children sleep while others are playing, provide a sleeping place a bit apart from the play space but still within your sight and hearing.

When setting up sleeping places for children, these strategies are very important:

**Be sure that each child sleeps in the same place each day.** Have an individual crib, cot, mat, or bed, and bedding for each child. This helps minimize the spread of head lice and infectious diseases. Label sleeping places and linens with children's names to reserve their use for individual children. Keep children's faces 3 feet apart to help stop the spread of diseases that travel through the air. (Sometimes this spacing can only be accomplished by putting children to sleep so that one child's head faces another child's feet.)

**Provide children with clean sheets and bedding.** Wash linens whenever they are soiled or wet. You should generally wash or send linens home for washing at least weekly. You may need to have linens for infants, toddlers, and twos washed more frequently. Store each child's bedding so that it does not touch another child's bedding.

**Make sure cribs and crib bedding are safe.** Many organizations, including the American Academy of Pediatrics, the National Institute of Child Health and Human Development (NICHD), and the U. S. Consumer Product Safety Commission, provide information on reducing the risk of Sudden Infant Death Syndrome (SIDS), also known as *crib death*. Know your state licensing requirements and consider taking a SIDS class if one is available in your area.

**Follow these guidelines to reduce the risk of SIDS:**[1]

- Use firm crib mattresses.

- Keep pillows, heavy blankets, comforters, stuffed toys, rattles, and squeeze toys out of cribs. Do not use bumper pads.

- Keep babies warm enough by dressing them in sleep clothes rather than by covering them with a blanket, because overheating seems to be one of the causes of SIDS. If you do use a blanket, use only a thin one.

- Make sure babies' heads and faces are uncovered while they sleep. If you use a blanket or top sheet, make sure that it does not reach higher than the baby's chest and that the end and sides of the covering are tucked under the crib mattress. Even so, blankets and sheets can accidently cover the baby's mouth and nose, so sleeping infants need to be checked.

- Watch for strangulation hazards. Make sure that there are no dangling cords from blinds, drapes, mobiles, or toys near the crib.

- Keep side rails up when children are in their cribs. Lower the mattress when children begin to sit or stand. Watch for signs that infants have outgrown their cribs, for instance, when they can pull themselves up by holding onto the railings. When cribs are no longer safe, move children to cots, mats, or beds.

**Do not put infants to sleep with a bottle.** Allowing children to have a bottle in their mouths while they are sleeping may cause the severe tooth decay known as *baby bottle mouth*. Drinking from a bottle during nap time can also cause choking and ear infections.

# Caring and Teaching

From birth, children differ in how much sleep they need, how soundly they sleep, and the regularity of their sleeping patterns. They also differ in how much time it takes them to fall asleep and wake up. Depending on their developmental levels and personal characteristics, children have a range of feelings about lying down to sleep and a variety of behaviors while waking up. Knowing how each child falls asleep and wakes can help you manage nap times with your group. Remember to talk to families about their sleeping routines at home and follow family practices when possible.

Here are some important things to do to help all children sleep and rest:

**Know each child's sleeping patterns, including how each child falls asleep and awakens.** Watch for cues that the child is sleepy. Infants communicate their need for sleep by crying, rubbing their eyes, or simply falling asleep wherever they are. Some children wake slowly, easing into the waking world, while others wake up quickly, cheerful and ready to go.

**Develop individualized, consistent nap time routines with children to help them fall asleep and wake up.** When you schedule nap time, think about scheduling it early enough in the day so that children are sleepy at their evening bedtimes.

**Make undressing and dressing a part of nap time.** Assist children as they practice these self-help skills, for example, by encouraging children to take off (or help take off) their shoes and socks. When it is time to put their shoes back on, they discover that the left shoe goes on the left foot, and the right one goes on the right foot.

**Avoid making nap time a battle.** Expect children to settle down at their own paces and respond appropriately to children who cry. Have alternative, quiet activities for children who do not sleep.

**Encourage families to bring comfort items from home.** Many children have a special "blankie" or other comfort item that they use to help them sleep. If you help children remember to take them home at night, they can have their special items to soothe them to sleep both at home and at your program. However, remember that toys and stuffed animals must not be placed in cribs.

**Take children outdoors each day.** Time in the fresh air and sunshine helps establish waking and sleeping patterns.

## Responding to What Children Need

Children's need for sleep changes as they develop. **Infants'** sleeping patterns change considerably during the first year. Young infants sleep for most of the day (and night). They sleep and wake, sleep and wake, sleep and wake. They typically develop a consistent sleep–wake cycle between 3 and 6 months of age. By the time they are 1 year old, they may take fewer and shorter naps during the day. While sleeping, infants often appear restless, twitch their arms and legs, smile, and suck.[2]

It is important to use these strategies with infants:

**Help infants learn to fall asleep on their own.** The National Sleep Foundation recommends that infants be put in their cribs when they are drowsy and about to fall asleep but before they fall totally asleep.[3] Infants put in their cribs this way learn to soothe themselves and fall back to sleep if they wake during the night.

**Put infants down to sleep on their backs.** The national "Back to Sleep" campaign has helped to dramatically reduce the incidence of SIDS. Once infants are able to turn over on their own, however, it is all right to let them stay on their tummies when they have turned over by themselves. When children are fully awake, use "tummy time" to help children develop the neck and back muscles they need so they can creep and crawl.

**Know strategies for helping children who have difficulty falling asleep.** Dr. Harvey Karp believes that infants have a "calming reflex,"[4] and that there are simple techniques for quickly calming even colicky babies. Learn how to soothe babies by swaddling and saying *shhh* rhythmically.

**Take babies out of their cribs as soon as they wake up.** Cribs are only for sleeping. Put babies on the floor for tummy time and provide other play and interactive experiences.

**Toddlers and twos** usually take one daily nap that lasts 1–3 hours. They nap on a cot or mat rather than in a crib. They communicate their need for sleep both verbally and nonverbally. Sometime during their second year, children change from sleeping in the morning and afternoon to sleeping only during the afternoon. As they develop, they may need more time to calm down and fall asleep, or they may rest without actually sleeping on some days. During this time, one nap might not be enough but two might be too many. This transitional period can be difficult. Remain flexible and plan your day to allow for one or two rest periods per day. Plan quiet time to help toddlers transition from active play to sleep, and prepare activities for children as they wake up. Remember that children still depend on you to help them regulate sleep and wakefulness.

Here are some strategies to use with toddlers and twos:

**Work with families** to coordinate when and how to move children from cribs to cots.

**Have a consistent place** for each child to sleep.

**Encourage children to bring comfort items,** such as blankets or stuffed animals, from home.

**Preschool** children still benefit from naps, although the length of time that they sleep or rest varies. While preschoolers sometimes resist napping, it is important for them to rest after an active morning and before an active afternoon. Here are some techniques that help preschool children settle down to nap:

**Plan a quiet activity** after lunch to help children relax. A story, fingerplay, quiet song, or other quiet music can help children transition from wakefulness to sleepiness.

**Establish a nap-time routine** that includes brushing teeth; toileting; setting up cots and mats if they are used; getting out bedding; taking off shoes; and going to their sleeping places with a book, quiet toy, or comfort item.

**Respect each child's individual pace.** Allow children to settle down and wake up at their own paces.

**Provide activities for children who wake up early or who do not sleep.** Some providers create "nap bags" with such things as books, small toys, crayons, and paper that children may bring to their cots or mats.

**School-age children** can learn about the importance of getting a good night's sleep, just as they can learn about other health habits. They are busy and active and may need some help relaxing from all of the demands on their energy: school, homework, friends, sports, and other activities and responsibilities.

School-age children may be arriving just as other children are waking up from naps. They can read to early risers, help preschool children fold their blankets, or just rest by themselves in a comfortable spot in your home.

When you help children rest and sleep, strengthening your relationship with them is as important as meeting their physical needs. As you interact with children during this routine, you show that you care about their well-being and security. Referring to the curricular objectives can help you to appreciate how sleeping and otherwise resting support children's development.

| What You Might Do | Why |
| --- | --- |
| Rock infants gently in your arms to help them begin to fall asleep, but put them in their cribs to soothe themselves to sleep. | When infants develop regular sleeping patterns and comfort themselves as they fall asleep, they are showing early signs of regulating their emotions and behaviors. *(Objective 1, Regulates own emotions and behaviors)* |
| Sing children's favorite lullabies, especially those that their families sing to them. Make sure that they have their safe comfort items with them. | A strong connection between children's homes and your program helps children feel cared about and secure. *(Objective 2, Establishes and sustains positive relationships)* |
| Respond to children's crying, eye rubbing, crankiness, or slowed activity by saying, "You're tired. It's time for you to take a nap." | This helps children make connections between cause and effect. It helps them begin to recognize and name their own fatigue and learn to solve the problem of being tired. *(Objective 12, Remembers and connects experiences)* |
| Ask a preschool child to use the toilet, wash hands, get a book, and lie down on his or her cot for nap time. | Preschool children are ready to follow more complex directions and participate fully in routines. *(Objective 1, Regulates own emotions and behaviors; Objective 3, Participates cooperatively and constructively in group situations; Objective 8, Listens to and understands increasingly complex language)* |
| Read the engaging rhymes in Mem Fox's *Time for Bed;* the classic *Good Night, Moon;* or *Hush, Little Baby* and its variations, *Hush, Little Alien* and *Hush, Little Dragon.* | When you read bedtime stories, you are not only helping a child fall asleep, you are introducing children to the joys of storytelling and the sounds of language. *(Objective 18, Comprehends and responds to books and other texts)* |

# Partnering With Families

Here are some strategies to help you work with families on sleeping and resting:

**Find out how each family handles naps and resting at home.** The "Family and Child Information Form" will help you gather information about each child's sleeping patterns and habits. Update it regularly. Learn about families' bedtime rituals and routines.

**Share daily information with parents about sleeping.** Encourage families to let you know if their child did not sleep well so you won't be surprised if you have a cranky child in your care. Likewise, let them know if their child did not sleep during the day or had a longer nap than usual. This information can help parents plan their evening routines.

**Have a clear policy about placing children on their backs to sleep and talk about your policy with families.** Be sure to let them know that you follow practices that reduce the risk of SIDS and encourage them to follow these practices at home. Hand out information from the American Academy of Pediatrics and other organizations that conduct the "Back to Sleep" campaign for safe sleeping. Reassure families that you give each infant "tummy time" when the baby is awake and you are watching. If the practice is new to a family, explain that it helps strengthen the baby's neck and shoulder muscles.

**Be aware of families' preferences for putting infants, toddlers, and twos to sleep.** Some families do not put young children to sleep in a separate room. They may not let children sleep alone and may let them stay awake until older children in the household go to sleep. Infants in some cultures are swaddled or put to sleep on bedboards. Find out about the sleeping practices your families follow with their children and, whenever possible and appropriate, incorporate them in your program.

**Work together to resolve differences.** Some families may ask you to limit the time their child sleeps at your program. Listen and gather information from family members. Share information about your views and experience. Then work out a plan that is acceptable to both you and the family.

**Offer resources to families who are concerned about sleeping issues.** Display books and articles. Encourage families to share their experiences with each other. Know when to suggest that a family talk to a doctor about a concern.

The following *LearningGames*® activities and the letter to families can help you build partnerships with families to make this routine beneficial for children. You use many of the same practices in your home, so families and you are truly partners in supporting children's learning and development.

## *LearningGames*® for Sleeping and Resting

Birth–12 months

### Game 4, "Soothing Your Baby"

Some babies fall asleep easily, but others have more difficulty. Simple techniques, including swaddling and making a rhythmic *shhh* sound (perhaps similar to the sound they hear in the womb), help babies learn to calm and soothe themselves.

12–24 months

### Game 42, "Make Undressing Easy"

When could be better than bedtime to help a child practice undressing? Encourage parents to play the game first with shoes and then socks, describing what their child is doing. "You took off your shoe! I think you can pull off your sock, too." Once shoes and socks are mastered, off come the pants (with a little help.) Add some words—*red pants*, *blue shirt*—to help children expand their vocabularies.

24–36 months

### Game 91, "Words for Time"

Many families have bedtime rituals, such as a bath and a story before bed. This *LearningGames* activity encourages families to talk with children about time the way you do. For example, they might say, "After your bath, we'll read a story. Then it will be time for bed." Talking about time helps children understand and predict what will come next in their own lives.

36–48 months

### Game 101, "Soap Curls"

Families can play this *LearningGames* activity to make bedtime baths even more fun—and to take away children's dread of washing hair. Thick shampoo lather can create new hairstyles for children to enjoy. They learn to feel comfortable with their images even as those images change.

48–60 months

### Game 159, "When, How, Why"

This *LearningGames* activity encourages families to ask *when, how,* or *why* questions while reading a bedtime story. Such questions support children's literacy skills. *LearningGames* activity 171, "Add to the Tale," also helps families find ways to make bedtime both relaxing and a time for learning.

[1] National Institute of Child Health and Human Development. (2003). *Safe sleep for your baby* (NIH Pub. No. 03-5355). Bethesda, MD: National Institutes of Health.

[2] National Sleep Foundation. (n.d.). *Children and sleep.* Retrieved January 24, 2009, from http://www.sleepfoundation.org/site/c.huIXKjM0IxF/b.4809577/k.BA8B/Children_and_Sleep.htm.

[3] Ibid.

[4] Karp, H. (2003). *The happiest baby on the block: The new way to calm crying and help your newborn baby sleep longer.* New York, NY: Bantam.

# A Letter to Families About Sleeping and Resting

Dear Families,

Every young child needs enough sleep during the day and at night for healthy growth and development. When children are rested, they enjoy and benefit from learning opportunities throughout the day. I want to know about your child's sleeping routines and habits at home. Sharing information will help me make sure that the sleeping routine I follow is consistent with what you do at home.

Here are some ways for us to work together:

- **Let me know your child's preferences.** It helps me understand what works and doesn't work at home. Are there special lullabies or words you child is used to hearing at bedtime? Do you read a story before your child goes to sleep?

- **Bring special items that comfort your child.** If your child has a special blanket or another object that makes falling asleep easier, please bring it. Please label it with your child's name and make sure I have it every day. We'll be careful not to lose it, and I'll help you remember to take it home at night.

- **Keep me informed about changes in your child's sleeping patterns.** Of course your child's sleeping patterns will change as he or she gets older. Let's coordinate changes, whether your child is making the big move from a crib to a bed or is no longer taking a morning nap.

- **Let me know if your child didn't sleep well the night before.** That way, I won't be surprised if your child is grumpy or sleepy. I can make changes in our schedule or activities if your child needs an earlier or longer nap. I'll let you know when and for how long your child naps each day here so you can adapt your evening plans, too.

- **Put your baby to sleep on his or her back.** This is a recommendation of the American Academy of Pediatrics and other national organizations to help prevent Sudden Infant Death Syndrome or SIDS (also known as *crib death*). Check their Web sites or ask me for information about "Back to Sleep" and what else you can do to reduce the risk of SIDS.

Together, we can make sleeping and resting a pleasant experience for your child.

Sincerely,

# Experiences

Every day in your program, you plan large periods during both the morning and afternoon for choice time and outdoor time. The 11 chapters in Part III describe the kinds of enjoyable experiences that engage children and support meaningful learning during those times. You will learn about the wide range of experiences you can offer to children: blocks, dramatic play, art, toys and games, stories and books, sand and water, discovery, music and movement, cooking, computers, and outdoor play. The materials you provide invite children to explore, discover, and learn about the world around them. Your purposeful interactions with children as they engage in these experiences reinforce and extend their learning. You use the teaching strategies described in chapter 4 to guide children's play and to make their learning meaningful.

Each of the chapters in part III includes lists of appropriate materials for different age-groups and examples of ways to enhance experiences by observing purposefully and responding thoughtfully to each child. We use the term *experiences*, rather than *activities*, to emphasize the importance of focusing attention on what the child is doing and experiencing. This often depends on the child's age, interests, temperament, and past experiences. Chapters 10–20 offer detailed guidance for basing your decisions about experiences on the characteristics that make each child unique.

One of the challenges of family child care is making experiences meaningful for children of very different ages and developmental levels. For example, during a single read-aloud session, you might encourage a young infant to pat the book, ask a mobile infant to point to the picture of the girl, laugh with a toddler when you use a deep voice for Papa Bear, prompt a preschool child to recall what the bears find when they look at their chairs, and ask a school-age child to imagine what Goldilocks will do after the written story ends. We therefore include a little story in each chapter to show how you might engage all of the children in the experiences you offer.

As in the chapters on routines, each chapter of part III concludes with suggestions for partnering with families by sharing related *LearningGames* and by sending a letter that explains the value of each type of experience. The game sheets and letters suggest ways for families to provide experiences at home that are similar to those you offer in your program.

# Blocks

**10**

# Blocks

---

Jorge (2 ½ years) and Rosa (4 years) help each other carry the basket of blocks into the center of the living room, where they dump it. "Make casa," announces Rosa as she starts to build an enclosure.

"Casa, casa", agrees Jorge, nodding his head as he begins to stack one block on top of another.

After watching the children build, you say, "I see you each built a house. Do you need a car so you can visit each other?"

Rosa gets two cars from the shelf and hands one to Jorge. He takes the car and pushes it along the floor. As she starts to lay blocks along the floor from her building to Jorge's, Rosa explains, "I make road."

---

Young children love playing with all kinds, sizes, and shapes of blocks. Because blocks are an open-ended material, children can use them in many different ways, from simply manipulating and carrying them to building increasingly complex structures. They can make models of the world around them and then use their creations as settings for dramatic play.

Blocks are ideal for promoting physical skills and eye–hand coordination. They are also designed to support mathematical thinking. Children learn the names of various shapes, create patterns, and compare the weights of different blocks. They begin to notice relative sizes, realizing, for example, that two square blocks can be positioned to serve as one longer block. Preschool and school-age children build intricate designs and buildings that represent places they have visited, such as a zoo or fire station. When children talk about what they are building, they develop oral language skills. When they ask you to help them make signs for their buildings, they are acquiring literacy skills.

# Setting Up for Block Play

Blocks appeal to most children. They are made from a variety of materials. Infants like to handle and mouth soft, spongy blocks. Toddlers delight in piling plastic and cardboard blocks on top of each other so they can knock them down. Preschoolers use hardwood unit or hollow blocks to make elaborate designs and to construct roads and buildings. The addition of props greatly expands the block play of preschool and school-age children.

## Choosing Blocks and Props

For younger children, look for blocks that are safe, soft, and washable:

- small and large foam blocks
- cloth-covered blocks
- small plastic blocks
- cardboard "brick" blocks with a coating that is easy to clean
- large interlocking plastic blocks
- small, wooden, colored table blocks of uniform size
- alphabet blocks
- colored 1-inch cubic blocks

Preschool and school-age children enjoy many of the blocks listed above, but they are ready for the challenge of hardwood blocks. There are two types:

- Unit blocks are made of hardwood and come in sets of proportional sizes and shapes (e.g., two triangular blocks equal one rectangular unit; two square blocks equal a longer rectangular unit, and so on). This design helps children understand math concepts as they select blocks, create designs, build, and sort the blocks during cleanup.
- Hollow blocks are large wooden pieces that come in five sizes and shapes: a half-square, a double square, two lengths of flat board, and a ramp. They are wonderful building materials for children to use outdoors or in a large indoor space.

Children can also build and construct with boxes. Collect sturdy cardboard boxes such as shoe boxes, oatmeal and salt containers, and gift and shipping boxes.

Simple props enhance children's block play. They can use them to decorate their block structures and for dramatic play. Garage and yard sales are a good place to find great buys on small toys that children enjoy using with blocks. Here are some items to collect:

- small wooden and plastic figurines of people and animals
- small cars and trucks
- miniature traffic signs
- dollhouse furniture
- paper towel rolls
- craft sticks
- rug samples
- shells, bottle caps, and other collectibles
- telephone wire

## Displaying Materials

Children can play with soft blocks anywhere: on a soft rug, a couch, or the floor. Small blocks can be used on a table or the floor. Unit blocks are best used on a wooden or linoleum floor, or a flat rug. You only need to provide children with enough space to play and a way to protect the buildings that older children make. One option is to protect a space for builders by the way you position a shelf or couch.

Especially if you have a separate space for your program, use shelves to define and protect a corner for building. A low shelf to hold blocks is ideal because arranging them by size and shape helps children find and return them. Label the place for each size and shape with a silhouette of the block cut from solidly colored contact paper.

Other storage options include plastic milk crates, a laundry basket, plastic dishpans, clear containers, and a wheeled cart.

# Caring and Teaching

Blocks support a broad range of creative, imaginative, constructive play. All children—boys and girls of all ages—should have uninterrupted time to build and create with blocks. As in all children's activities, your interest and involvement helps children get the most benefit from their play.

## Responding to Each Child

Take time to observe children as they play. Notice what kinds of blocks they prefer, what discoveries they make, the kinds of structures they build, and whether they work alone or with others. Refer to the curricular objectives and reflect on what each child is doing and learning so you can respond in ways that support and extend children's ideas.

**Infants** explore and learn about the world through their senses, and they are likely to put everything in their mouths. Mobile infants enjoy climbing over large blocks as much as stacking them and pushing them over.

| Observe | Reflect | Respond |
|---|---|---|
| With both hands, Jeremy grasps a sponge block you handed to him and examines it visually. He looks at you, gives it back, and laughs when you nod and say, "Thank you, Jeremy." Then he immediately reaches for it again. When Tamika comes by, he hands one to her and smiles when she gives it back to him. | Jeremy is grasping and releasing objects. *(Objective 7, Demonstrates fine motor strength and coordination)*<br><br>He enjoys being with adults and other children. *(Objective 2, Establishes and sustains positive relationships)* | Repeat this game with Jeremy, using smaller objects so he learns to grasp objects of various sizes. "Here's a block for you. Here's another one. Now you have two blocks."<br><br>Include other children in the games so he continues to take an interest in and feel comfortable playing with children of different ages. |

**Toddlers and twos** enjoy blocks they can manipulate, carry, and use to build towers and roads. They stack colorful plastic blocks and large foam blocks and lay them along the floor. Cardboard blocks with a brick pattern are easy to stack, and they are sturdy enough for toddlers to sit or walk on them. Twos are ready for the challenge of building more carefully with small wooden blocks of uniform sizes and shapes. Children this age like to show you what they are doing with blocks. Their favorite activity is to build a tower, knock it down, and then rebuild it—again and again!

| Observe | Reflect | Respond |
| --- | --- | --- |
| Tamika is playing with foam blocks. She puts one block on top of another until they are almost ready to fall. Then she pushes them over, scattering them across the room. She collects the blocks, builds again, knocks them down, and repeats the sequence four times. | Tamika is able to continue a task entirely on her own for more than 10 minutes. *(Objective 11, Demonstrates positive approaches to learning)*<br><br>She carefully places the blocks to make towers. *(Objective 7, Demonstrates fine motor strength and coordination)* | Talk about what Tamika is doing to show her that you are interested: "You're having a great time with those blocks, Tamika! You are stacking them and knocking them down."<br><br>Suggest other ways to use the blocks when Tamika seems finished with this game: "Let's see what else we can do. We can make a road for a toy car." |

**Preschool children** make towers, roads, and enclosures with blocks. They are more likely to name their buildings and use them as settings for dramatic play. For example, they might create a zoo that is complete with animals in separate enclosures and with a parking lot.

They also create designs and patterns with blocks. Because you probably cannot leave these block creations in place, try to have a camera handy to take pictures. Display the photos of children's work and share them with families. You will be amazed how this acknowledgment of their effort inspires children to create more complex designs and buildings with the blocks you provide for them. To encourage preschool children to use blocks and learn from their play, help them plan their buildings and suggest new ideas when they are ready for greater challenges.

| Observe | Reflect | Respond |
|---|---|---|
| Rosa makes an enclosure of blocks and carefully places some STYROFOAM™ pieces inside. When you ask her what she is making, she explains, "Make bake shop. Papa work." | Rosa is recreating a place she has visited with her father. *(Objective 12, Remembers and connects experiences)*<br><br>She uses blocks to make a store and STYROFOAM™ to represent food. *(Objective 14, Uses symbols and images to represent something not present)* | Expand on what Rosa has said to help her learn more English: "You made the bakery where your papa works. He bakes very good bread and cakes."<br><br>Extend her idea by pretending with her. Ask, "Rosa, may I buy some bread from you?" |

**School-age children** want high-level challenges when they use blocks, as do some older preschoolers. They might make intricate designs with variously shaped blocks or create a model of a city block with stores, apartment buildings, and streets. Block building is an excellent way for children to learn about structures and mapping. School-age children often like to work on a project over time, coming back to it over several days. This can be a challenge in family child care because it is not always possible to protect their work. If they are using table blocks, you might provide sturdy cardboard or a piece of wood on which to build so their projects can be moved to a protected storage place. You can inspire school-age children to use blocks by taking an interest and challenging them with new ideas.

| Observe | Reflect | Respond |
| --- | --- | --- |
| Tyrone calls you over to show you a very intricate design he has made with colored, variously shaped blocks. "Look what I made! This is my best design ever. I really want to show it to my dad." | Tyrone's design really is amazing. It's very clear that he is proud of what he made, as he should be.<br><br>I want to honor his creation and challenge him a little. | Comment on what he did: "You spent a lot of time on this design. I think it's the most detailed one you ever made! Let's definitely protect it until your Dad has seen it."<br><br>Provide a challenge: "I wonder if you can recreate it on the computer with the new program that lets you move shapes around." |

## Engaging Children of All Ages

Although the children in your family child care home are at very different stages in their block play, it's possible to involve them all in using blocks. Here's an example of how this might happen.

"May I get out the blocks?" asks Keisha (4 ½ years). "I want to make a road for cars and a drawbridge like the one we went on near the beach. I don't want the little kids to knock it down."

You offer, "I'll help you arrange some couch pillows to create a place for you to build."

Keisha is delighted and starts to build with the wooden blocks, carefully taking them out of the large basket she used to carry them. Jorge (2 ½ years) wants to build, too, but he's happy to use the alphabet blocks on the rug. Nathan (3 years) sees what Keisha is doing. He asks, "Me he'p?"

"Okay, but only if you are careful," replies Keisha. "Don't let the little kids come in here while we're building. You can make the road for the cars."

Keisha and Nathan begin to work together as you change Tamika's (19 months) diaper and bring her into the center of the living room, where Jorge has begun playing with the alphabet blocks. Tamika heads right for the block that Jorge is adding to a stack. He holds it up before she can get it.

"Jorge doesn't want you to take his block," you explain to Tamika. "I have some blocks for you, too," you say, offering her a basket with foam blocks. Tamika happily dumps the blocks and begins to play with them as Jorge moves his blocks to another part of the rug. "There are plenty of blocks for everyone," you assure them.

"I need a piece of string," says Keisha, "so I can make the drawbridge go up and down. Nathan, you get the cars and traffic signs."

"I think we can find some string," you respond, picking Jeremy up and carrying him to the kitchen to find some. Nathan collects cars and traffic signs from the shelf. Returning from the kitchen, you hand Keisha the string. "Here you are, Keisha. I can't wait to see how you make the drawbridge!"

This example shows how you might promote block play for children of different ages. It illustrates several points:

- When you make a variety of blocks available, children of different ages all have materials to use safely.
- Open-ended materials like blocks challenge children to practice their skills in creative ways.
- Infants need to be protected when they are near older children who are using blocks.
- Older children sometimes need you to help preserve their buildings by providing a protected place for them to build.
- Displaying toys in containers on a low shelf makes it easy for children to find what they need on their own.

# Partnering With Families

Families will be interested in knowing what their children are doing and learning when they play with blocks. The following *LearningGames®* activities and the letter to families about blocks are ways to share that information.

## *LearningGames®* for Blocks

### 12–24 months

**Game 53, "Build Together"**

Encourage the family to build alongside their child, copying their child's movements and describing what they and the child are doing. First the child is the leader. Later the child follows an adult's directions. Children learn many things as they play with blocks, for example, to make patterns, to explain how two buildings are the same, and to follow directions. Demonstrate how you play this game with their child.

### 24–36 months

**Game 78, "Building Blocks"**

Blocks come in many shapes and sizes. In this activity, children explore and experiment with blocks on their own. With practice, children learn how to place blocks in long lines on the floor and, later, how to stack them so they will not topple over. Share the kinds of things you say to children as they build with blocks, for example, "You made a very tall building," or "I see that you used three different kinds of blocks today." Encourage family members to share examples of how their children respond to comments and questions during block play at home.

36–48 months

### Game 119, "Two-Step Directions"

This game is especially good to repeat over the course of a year or more so children have the opportunity to follow directions in many situations. One way to play is to have children follow instructions for building with blocks. For example, you might direct, "Take five blocks from the shelf and make a long road." This is also a good game for cleaning blocks up. Suggest, "Put the big blocks away first. Then put the little blocks where they belong." With practice, children progress from following two-step directions to following three- or even four-step directions.

---

48–60 months

### Game 174, "Which Is Best?"

Encourage the family to help their child learn to solve problems by offering two possible solutions and letting the child choose an option. Give an example from your own work with children: "When a block tower keeps falling, I might say, 'You are frustrated because that tower keeps falling. What will you do next? You could build the next tower wider at the bottom. You could also decide to build something else. Which idea would you like to try?'"

# A Letter to Families About Blocks

Dear Families,

Blocks are among children's favorite toys. I provide several different kinds of blocks. The babies touch, squeeze, and throw soft spongy blocks. Older children build with wooden blocks on the table or floor. They use larger blocks to make tall towers and settings for their pretend play.

When children build with blocks, they learn about sizes, shapes, colors, and why it's important to build on a sturdy base if they want their structures to stand. Sometimes they build alone, creating designs with the blocks. Sometimes they work together to build something they have seen, such as a fire station or a school. Then they use it to pretend. This is one way children represent the world around them and learn more about it.

I talk to the children about their constructions as they play with blocks. I describe what I see and ask questions to encourage them to think about what they are doing. My questions also encourage them to express their ideas in words. I might say,

> "You like to build with the blocks and then knock them down."

> "I see that you made a road for your car. What will happen when the car runs out of gas? Do you need a gas station?"

> "You made an interesting pattern with the blocks. It goes: red square, blue triangle; red square, blue triangle; red square…I wonder what comes next."

As your child plays with blocks at home, your comments and questions can extend his or her ideas.

Here are some other suggestions for block play at home:

- Consider the age of your child as you choose from the many different kinds of blocks that are available:
  - Select soft and safe blocks for your baby. Foam, cloth, and plastic blocks are best for this age.
  - Toddlers and twos can use a great variety of blocks. Colored wooden table blocks and alphabet, foam, cardboard, and plastic blocks are all appropriate.
  - Preschool and school-age children like to create all kinds of structures with wooden blocks in proportional sizes. They also like to make designs with colorful pattern blocks.
- Store small blocks in containers like plastic tubs or shoe boxes, and label them with a picture and words. Then your child will be able to find what he or she needs and put the blocks away after playing with them.

Sincerely,

# Dramatic Play

# 11

# Dramatic Play

Rosa (4 years) and Keisha (4 ½ years) excitedly open the clinic prop box you put together after Rosa's mother told you about their visit to the clinic. They look through its contents. "¡El estetoscopio"! exclaims Rosa, pulling out the stethoscope.

Keisha takes out a prescription pad and pretends to write, saying, "I'm gonna write a 'scription for some medicine. You have to take this to the drugstore," she adds, looking at you.

Jeremy (8 months) crawls over to the box and starts pulling things out. Keisha pushes him away and says, "Go away, Jeremy. You can't play with us."

Jeremy screams. Picking him up, you say, "Jeremy, you're interested in the box, too. What is in the box for Jeremy?"

"Here," says Keisha handing you a roll of gauze. "He can have this."

Jeremy sits on your lap and happily pulls on the gauze, watching it unroll, as Rosa and Keisha begin to enact a medical check-up. "Jeremy can be our patient," says Keisha.

When children engage in pretend or dramatic play, they use what they know and often show how they feel about experiences they have had. As they pretend, they gain a deeper understanding of their experiences. They recall something that happened, take on a role, and fit the experience with other experiences and knowledge. Dramatic play evolves gradually from the imitation and exploration of infants, toddlers, and twos to the imaginative, symbolic, and more social play of preschool and school-age children.

High levels of dramatic play are evident when children begin to explore less familiar roles, use imaginary props instead of real ones, and engage in conversation about their play. Play episodes may extend over several days. They are learning how to work with others, use language to accomplish a task, control their behavior, negotiate roles, take the perspectives of other persons, and solve problems. These self-regulation skills are critical for school readiness and successful learning.[1] Some children need adult support to engage in mature play.

# Setting Up for Dramatic Play

There is no need to spend a lot of money on fancy props. Basics are enough to inspire children to pretend. A collection of "beautiful junk" can substitute for other objects. For example, paper towel rolls can become telescopes; a bead strung on yarn can be a stethoscope; blocks can be transformed into cars; a cardboard box can be a crib for a doll or be a house. As children begin to think more abstractly, their props become less realistic and sometimes entirely imaginary.

## Choosing Props

You can inspire pretend play by providing props, such as cups and pots for sand and water play, and rolling pins, cookie cutters, and plastic knives for playdough activities. While playing with water and cups, two preschool children may pretend that they are pouring soda and begin playing restaurant. A child rolling playdough might exclaim, "Watch out for my snake! He might bite you!"

The type of props you provide influences children's pretend play. Realistic props encourage children to act out familiar, everyday roles. Preschool and school-age children often explore more fantasy roles when props are nonrealistic. Dolls that reflect the ethnicities of the children in your care promote children's positive social–emotional development and encourage children to act out home scenarios. Puppets and flannel board figures also encourage imaginary play and language development.

When you create a special place with props for dramatic play, the children will probably engage in even more pretend play. A simple collection of props for dramatic play includes the following:

- stuffed animals and soft baby dolls
- life-like dolls that reflect the ethnicities of the children
- doll bottles, baby blankets, a cradle, and a doll bed
- dress-up clothes such as hats, jackets, shoes, and pocketbooks
- push-and-pull toys like a baby carriage, shopping cart, and lawn mower
- telephones (play or disconnected real phones; traditional and cellular phones)
- pots, pans, and plastic dishes and utensils
- plastic, rubber, or wooden cars and trucks
- child-sized broom, dustpan, and mop
- assorted plastic containers and empty food boxes

By age 4, children's dramatic play moves from household themes to reenacting other experiences. To encourage mature play, you can put together prop boxes. A prop box is a collection of objects related to a particular topic. To collect items for prop boxes, ask families for donations, check garage sales, and try secondhand stores. Simple materials are best. Your goal is for children to use their imaginations as much as possible instead of relying on realistic props.

Here are a few ideas for prop boxes:

### Hospital or clinic

white or green shirts, or old scrubs

stethoscope

gauze and Band-Aids®

prescription pads (small pads of paper) and pencils

tape measure

eye chart

height chart

scale

### Supermarket

toy cash register, play money, credit cards (junk mail samples or cards from closed accounts)

empty food containers

plastic fruits and vegetables

paper bags

balance scale made with margarine tubs and string

coupons

supermarket ads and signs

### Shoe store

assorted shoes

shoe boxes

shoeshine kit with clear polish, brush, and rags

foot measure (from a shoe store) or rulers

toy cash register with play money and credit cards

### Post office

sample charts from the local post office

junk mail, letters, cards

envelopes, stationery

pencils and pens

ink pads and stamps (for example, *First Class, Priority Mail, Next Day*)

stickers (to serve as stamps) and address labels

signs (for example, *Open, Closed, Stamps*)

### Beautiful junk

scraps of wood

empty spools

cardboard

a variety of fabrics

STYROFOAM™

construction paper

straws

pipe cleaners

yarn

tape

scissors

pencils, crayons, and markers

## Displaying Materials

Although dramatic play can take place anywhere in your home or outdoors, you may be able to have a special place for furniture, props, and dress-up clothes. A card table with a sheet over it becomes a cozy playhouse, an interesting cave, or a camping tent. Cardboard boxes and plastic or wooden crates can be painted and turned into pretend appliances such as a stove, a sink, and a refrigerator. You can often find these items at yard sales. A corner of the living room or playroom might become a dramatic play area. If you use a separate part of your home for your program, a shelf and furniture can be used to define the space for dramatic play and to store props.

Here are some ideas for storing and displaying props and materials:

- plastic containers with lids to hold props with many parts
- wooden pegs on a board for hanging clothes, hats, and pocketbooks
- a shoe bag for shoes and other small items
- a small coatrack, cut down if necessary to fit the children's reach, for hanging dress-up clothes
- three-tiered wire baskets that hang from a hook to hold empty food containers, ties and scarves, costume jewelry, and doll clothes
- a board with hooks or pegs to hang pots, pans, cooking utensils, mops, brooms, and dress-up clothes

# Caring and Teaching

While props are valuable for inspiring children to pretend, your interest in their play and your active support are even more important. When you play pat-a-cake or peek-a-boo with an infant, pretend to talk on a phone with a toddler, provide real (but safe) tools and encourage a 2-year-old to "fix" a table, have tea with a preschooler, or watch a puppet show staged by a school-age child, you are encouraging children to engage in dramatic play.

## Responding to Each Child

Throughout each day, you have to decide when to participate in children's pretend play and when your interaction is not needed. Your ongoing observations will help you determine whether your active involvement, just a few suggestions, or some thoughtful questions are needed to extend a child's ideas. When you do participate in children's play, avoid trying to take over and direct the play. Children often play very well on their own, and that is your goal.

**Infants** are much more interested in interacting with you than in playing with any toy or prop. Young infants imitate facial expressions, environmental sounds, and some of the actions they see as they watch others. Games such pat-a-cake and rolling a ball back and forth teach infants how much fun it is to play with others. Later, usually between 9–15 months, infants begin to repeat actions they have seen others perform in the past. For example, a child might touch a comb to her head, imitating what an older child did the day before.

As you observe children imitating and pretending, think about the objectives for learning and development that apply to children birth to age 6. Reflect on what each child is learning so you can respond in ways that support and extend his or her play.

| Observe | Reflect | Respond |
| --- | --- | --- |
| Jeremy looks at you as you change his diaper and sing his favorite song, "The Wheels on the Bus." He waves his arms and says, "Ba-ba. Ba-ba-ba," with a big smile on his face. | Jeremy is responding to a familiar song. (*Objective 34, Explores musical concepts and expression*)<br><br>He is communicating with me by vocalizing. (*Objective 9, Uses spoken language to express thoughts and needs*) | Repeat his speech sounds: "I hear you saying, 'Ba-ba. Ba-ba-ba.' Are you singing with me, Jeremy?"<br><br>Continue the experience of singing and gesturing: "This is your favorite song. Let's sing it again. 'Oh, the wheels on the bus go round and round....'" |

**Toddlers** are often content to play on their own. A child might cover a doll with a blanket and say, "Night, night," or pick up a telephone and say, "Hello. Good-bye," seemingly to no one in particular. They sometimes use props to enact simple routines, such as combing a doll's hair or feeding a bottle to a doll. As they get to be **2 years old**, you may see them substitute one object for another while they pretend, such as using a ring from a stacking toy as a bagel or pushing a block along the floor as if it were a car. The size and shape of the objects suggest what they represent. As their language skills develop, twos engage in coordinated play. For example, two children might play side by side, both pretending to be firefighters and taking turns using the hose.

| Observe | Reflect | Respond |
| --- | --- | --- |
| Tamika is pushing an empty doll carriage around your living room. She sees a doll on the floor, picks it up, and places it in the carriage. Noticing a small blanket on the floor, she tries to pick it up, but it is stuck under the leg of a chair. She pulls at it, pushes the chair away to release the blanket, and picks it up. | Tamika is beginning to engage in pretend play. *(Objective 14, Uses symbols and images to represent something not present)*<br><br>She encountered a problem and figured out a way to solve it entirely on her own. *(Objective 11, Demonstrates positive approaches to learning)* | Describe what she has done: "That blanket was stuck under the chair, but you figured out how to get it. You solved the problem!"<br><br>Encourage her pretend play: "I see you are taking the baby for a ride in the carriage. Are you going to cover your baby with the blanket? You don't want the baby to get cold." |

**Preschool children** can and should reach a mature level of pretend play called *sociodramatic play*. As discussed in the "Applying Research to Practice" section, children develop self-regulation skills as they play, and those skills are necessary for academic success. Sociodramatic play requires children to cooperate and pretend with others. It is characterized by six skills:[3]

1. role-playing: assigning and assuming roles

2. using props: using objects to represent other objects or substituting words and actions for objects

3. making believe: acting out real or imaginary events or actions

4. persisting: engaging in pretend play for at least 10 minutes

5. interacting: engaging in cooperative play efforts

6. communicating verbally: talking about play scenarios

Encourage preschool children to take on different roles, work together, make believe about situations they have experienced, and sustain their play.

| Observe | Reflect | Respond |
| --- | --- | --- |
| Keisha is setting a table for a tea party as Rosa watches. Keisha says, "I need three cups and three saucers for me, Rosa, and Nathan. One, two, three." Then she pretends to pour tea into each cup and asks, "Do you want sugar in your tea?" | Keisha counts correctly to three, using one number for each object. *(Objective 20, Uses number concepts and operations)* She is making believe about situations. *(Objective 14, Uses symbols and images to represent something not present)* | Extend her ideas by asking questions: "Do you have enough teacups and saucers for Jorge and me to join you? How many cups and saucers will you need when we do?" Provide opportunities and objects for her to count (up to five), for example, setting the table for lunch, and sorting and counting collectibles. |

After a day at school, **young school-age children** often enjoy pretending with younger children. By engaging with younger children, they teach them the skills involved in mature play, such as taking on a role and using imaginary props.

**Older school-age children** will probably be less interested in playing with preschool children. Their pretend play is likely to be more formal and planned. For example, they may write their own scripts, make costumes, rehearse, and perform their plays for you and the younger children. They might also reenact scenes they have seen on television. School-age children need your encouragement and help with finding the materials they need.

| Observe | Reflect | Respond |
|---|---|---|
| Tyrone brings a marionette he received for his birthday. "Watch this," he says. "I know how to work the strings to make my puppet dance. Isn't it awesome? I'll put on a puppet show for the other kids when I get back from school." | Manipulating a marionette is quite challenging. It's great that Tyrone wants to put on a puppet show for the other children. | Validate his new skills: "It's not easy to make a marionette dance. You must have been practicing! I see you taught yourself how to do it." Support his idea by suggesting, "We have some hand puppets, too. After your show, will you help Keisha and Rosa put on a show?" |

## Engaging Children of All Ages

Although the children in your care are at very different stages in their dramatic play, it's possible to involve all of them in using props to pretend. Here is an example.

Knowing that Rosa's (4 years) uncle is a painter, you ask him to help you put a painter's prop box together. When you bring it out, Rosa investigates its contents. She pulls out a painter's hat and puts it on.

You respond, "Yes, Rosa, your uncle is a painter. He wears a hat just like that. I asked him to help us because he knows just what a painter uses. Do you know what? My dining room table needs some fresh paint. Will you paint it for me?"

Rosa asks, "Color?"

You continue to encourage her play by asking, "What colors do you have?"

"Mira", says Rosa, pulling the paint samples out of the box.

You respond, "Oh, my! Look at all of those colors! I think this blue will go well with my curtains."

Nathan (3 years) has been watching you and Rosa carefully. He pulls out another painter's hat and puts it on his head. He announces, "Me paint!"

"Okay, Mr. Painter," you tell Nathan. "Here's a paintbrush and bucket for you. Will you please paint my chairs?"

While Rosa and Nathan are playing painter, Keisha (4 ½ years) draws a picture, and Jorge builds with colored blocks.

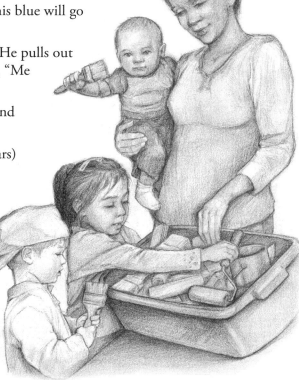

When Jeremy (8 months) wakes up from his nap, you change his diaper and bring him into the dining room, where the painters are still busy. Jeremy watches the action with interest, and you describe what is going on. "See what Rosa and Nathan are doing? They are painting my furniture with big brushes."

Jeremy reaches for the brush that Rosa is using. You find the paint roller in the prop box and prompt Rosa, "I wonder how to use this roller."

Rosa takes the roller and hands Jeremy the brush. "I use," she explains.

"Let's take your brush over here," you tell Jeremy as you move to the couch, where you can hold him as you talk with Keisha and Jorge (2 ½ years).

When Tyrone returns from school later that afternoon, he notices the new prop box. As he looks through it, he exclaims, "Hey, this is cool!"

You ask, "Would you like to fill the buckets with water and take them outside to paint the fence? We're just about ready to go outside." Tyrone thinks it's a great idea and agrees with your suggestion to have the other children join him.

This is an example of how you might encourage dramatic play with children of different ages by providing a box of props. It illustrates several points:

- Your involvement in children's play is very important.

- You do not have to involve all of the children in the same activity at one time. Children should have choices about what to do.

- Each child can participate in the play at his or her own level. A mobile infant may be content with sensory exploration of the props while the older children use them for make-believe.

- Simple materials can support important learning.

# Partnering With Families

You do not need fancy props to inspire children to play, especially if the props represent things they know from their own experiences. Families can be a great resource in preparing prop boxes, and they will be more willing to help you if they understand the value of dramatic play in their child's development and learning. The following *LearningGames*® activities and the letter to families about dramatic play can help you share information.

## LearningGames® for Dramatic Play

### Birth–12 months

### Game 26, "Imitating Actions"

Explain to families that you often play imitation games with the children in your family child care program because imitation is an important form of early learning. When you give this game to an infant's parent, describe some actions that the child likes to imitate when he or she is with you.

___

### 12–24 months

### Game 37, "Animal Sounds"

In this fun game, children imitate the sounds that we say animals make, for example, "The dog says, 'Woof, woof.'" Families can play this game with toy animals, with pictures, or with books. They can play it again and again, adding new animals each time. In addition to making animal sounds, children can name the animals. Share with families any animal sounds you have noticed their child imitating in your program.

___

24–36 months

### Game 71, "Dress-Up Play"

When you give families this game, explain that it will give them ideas about how to talk with children as they dress up and how to change dress-up items occasionally so that children have some new choices as time passes. Model and talk about how you do this in your dramatic play space.

36–48 months

### Game 147, "Props for Pretending"

Tell families that they can make prop boxes at home that are similar to the ones that you have in family child care. Help families understand how to select props related to themes. This *LearningGames* activity offers several ideas for getting started.

48–60 months

### Game 189, "Let's Imagine"

Older 4-year-olds enjoy playing this game with their families. Point out the "Ready to Move On" circle at the end of the game and let families know that you would love to see some of the stories they record. Share with a family what their child does in your program.

[1] Elias, C. L., & Berk, L. E. Self-regulation in young children: Is there a role for sociodramatic play? *Early Childhood Research Quarterly, 17*(2), 216–238.

[2] Berk, L.E., & Winsler, A. (1995). *Scaffolding children's learning: Vygotsky and early childhood education.* Washington, DC: National Association for the Education of Young Children.

[3] Smilansky, S., & Shefatya, L. (1990). *Facilitating play: A medium for promoting cognitive, socio-emotional, and academic development in young children.* Gaithersburg, MD: Psychological and Educational Publications.

# A Letter to Families About Dramatic Play

Dear Families,

Dramatic play is one of the ways children gain a better understanding of their experiences. In dramatic play, children take on different roles, act out real or imaginary situations, use props to make believe, and work together. They learn to cooperate with others, solve problems, and control their own behavior—all of which are important skills for school success. When children pretend, they recall experiences and agree on how to re-create them. To play the role of a doctor, they have to remember what a doctor does, what tools a doctor uses, how a doctor examines a patient, and what a doctor might say.

Every day, I play games like peek-a-boo with the babies and encourage them to imitate simple actions. I make believe with toddlers and twos as they play with dolls, push cars along the floor, or pretend to be a cat. I observe the preschool children to see what interests them, and I provide simple props related to topics they are talking about. Sometimes I join in their play without taking over. We all enjoy the plays and puppet shows our school-age children plan and put on for us.

Because dramatic play can take place anywhere and at any time, you probably already encourage this type of play at home. The simple imitation games you play with your baby while changing a diaper or during bath time are two examples. Soon your child learns to pretend to be a noisy puppy, a mommy or daddy caring for a baby, or a firefighter putting out fire. Dramatic play becomes much more complex as your child gains more experience and develops skills to pretend.

Here are some ways to support your child's dramatic play:

- **Talk about real-life experiences as they take place.** On a trip to the grocery store, post office, or clinic, talk about what is happening. Explain what people are doing, their jobs, and the names of tools and other objects they use. This helps your child understand and recall those experiences in pretend play.

- **Provide props that inspire pretend play.** Dolls, doll blankets, a cradle, telephones, pots, pans, plastic dishes, and safe tools will encourage your child to explore social roles. Other useful props include people and animal figurines; transportation toys such as cars, trucks, and boats; and various ride-on toys.

- **Make believe with your child.** This is one of the best ways to encourage your child to pretend. You can also encourage pretend play by asking questions; providing dress-up clothes and work-related props such as firefighter hats, work gloves, and a toy stethoscope; and taking on a role, yourself.

- **Encourage your school-age child's imaginative play.** Your child might enjoy creating plays and acting them out, or using puppets to retell a story.

Sincerely,

# Art

**12**

# Art

At the easel one morning, Rosa (4 years) paints what she identifies as a "purple pumpkin." After overhearing Rosa, Keisha (4 ½ years) comes to you, rather upset. She declares, "Pumpkins are orange. Everybody knows that." You explain, "That's true, Keisha. There *are* orange pumpkins. But it's fine if Rosa paints a purple pumpkin because she likes the way it looks. She is using her imagination! You are also free to paint a pumpkin purple, blue, green, orange, or *any* color. When you paint, you're in charge!"

As Rosa's pumpkin painting illustrates, art is a means of self-expression. When children scribble with a jumbo crayon, poke holes in playdough, or glue a leaf to cardboard, they communicate their feelings and ideas. They may use bright colors to express excitement and draw a sun to communicate their joy. Through their creations, children represent the world around them. It is a way of expressing themselves that is as powerful as anything they could ever say or write.

Young children also want to explore art materials without necessarily representing anything in particular or being concerned about a final product. Children use most—and sometimes all—of their senses during art experiences, especially touch and sight. They are learning how to control art media and tools, so experimentation is often more important to them than what they make.

Art also helps children acquire academic skills. Children represent their thoughts and ideas by painting, drawing, sculpting, and constructing. They learn about language and literacy as they sign their names to their creations and read along as you record what they tell you about their artwork. Children learn math concepts as they explore patterns and spatial relationships in their work. They explore scientific concepts firsthand as they mix paints together, watch clay harden, and balance mobiles. They learn about social studies as they recycle materials and pay attention to the art of various cultures. Art is a way of learning.

# Setting Up for Art

Wherever you have a child-sized table and chairs in your home is probably the most convenient place for children to draw, paste collages, and play with clay. Alternatively, you can use booster seats or phone books to seat children at your kitchen or dining room table. Floors can be protected with newspaper, old shower curtains, vinyl tablecloths, or painters' drop cloths. Many young children like sitting on the floor while they work.

Painting near a sink is wise because cleanup is easier near a water source. You can make tabletop easels from large wallpaper-sample books or cardboard boxes. Use clothespins or binder clips to hold paper in place. Make a wall easel by tacking a large piece of plastic to a wall and placing newspaper or a drop cloth on the floor to collect drips. Large sheets of paper can be taped on the protected wall. Because painting can be a social experience, you may want to invest in a freestanding, double-sided easel. Easels can be set up in areas away from furniture, preferably on linoleum, tile, or wooden floors that can be wiped easily. No matter where children paint, you will want to protect the floor. Have smocks nearby for painting and other messy art activities. In nice weather, easels and art tables can be moved outside for different sensory experiences.

## Choosing Materials

Think about all of the children in your program. What do they enjoy most? What new skills are they developing? Who enjoys messy activities? Who avoids them? This information will help you decide what materials are appropriate and how to prepare the environment.

### Infants, Toddlers, and Twos

Infants, toddlers, and twos like to experiment with art materials, watching the effects of their actions.

For *finger painting,* young children can

- spread paint on tabletops that are protected by securing plastic wrap with tape, on trays, or on mirrors with smooth edges
- use nontoxic shaving cream or mud instead of traditional finger paints, either at room temperature or slightly warmed (A dab of pudding on a high-chair tray provides finger painting fun for babies without any danger of the children's ingesting something harmful.)

A word about using food for art: Food can often be part of a valuable art experience, so using it might enhance your art program. As noted above, giving babies pudding to smear with their hands is a safe sensory experience. Macaroni can be dyed and strung as a necklace, and beet juice is a vibrant natural dye for fabrics. We add a word of caution, though. Because many people throughout the world do not have enough to eat, some families find it wasteful—even disrespectful—to use food for anything but nutritional purposes. You want to be thoughtful about others' views. Find out what the families of the children in your program think about using food in art experiences and plan accordingly.

For *painting with water,* young children can

- use household paintbrushes to cover the outside walls of your home, sidewalks, and tree trunks with water
- use stubby-handled brushes (5–6 inches long), which are easier for young painters to use

For *painting with tempera,* young children can

- use flat brushes (5–6 inches long) with nylon bristles and thick, stubby handles
- try other painting tools
    - empty deodorant bottles with rollers
    - squeeze bottles
    - dishwashing pom-poms
    - rollers
    - spray bottles
    - cotton swabs
- experiment with a variety of papers (about 24 inches by 36 inches, or larger)
    - newsprint
    - paper bags
    - paper towels
    - butcher paper of various sizes and shapes
    - wallpaper samples
    - paper plates
    - irregular paper donated by a local printer

For *drawing*, young children can

- use a variety of tools
  - jumbo crayons
  - jumbo chalk
  - water-based markers
  - soap crayons
  - scribble wafers

- use a variety of writing surfaces, such as a sidewalk or blacktop, as well as different kinds of paper

For *molding*, young children can

- use homemade playdough, which is cheaper and less messy than purchased doughs, or use ready-made doughs (Basic dough can be made by mixing 3 cups of flour, 1 cup of salt, 1/4 cup of salad oil, and 1 cup of water. Add food coloring to the water, or have children use an eyedropper to add liquid food coloring to the dough and then work the dye in with their hands.)

- use basic tools for pounding, poking, rolling, and stamping the dough
  - wooden mallets
  - craft sticks
  - wooden or plastic rods cut to 6-inch lengths
  - potato mashers

For *collages*, any nontoxic items that will stick to paper with library paste will engage toddlers and twos, but do not offer items on which children can choke. Young children can

- use items such as these:
  - ribbons
  - papers of assorted textures and colors
  - magazines and catalogs
  - fabric scraps
  - nontoxic leaves, dried flowers, and weeds
  - photographs
  - gift wrap
  - greeting cards, postcards, and business cards

## Preschool and School-Age Children

Preschool and school-age children can use all of the materials you offer to the younger children plus variations that will extend their ideas. Think about the children in your care and decide which of the following art experiences will interest them.

For *painting*, preschool and school-age children can

- use flat or round brushes with metal bands and no seams
- experiment with these media
    - liquid tempera
    - poster paint
    - watercolors
    - finger paint
    - water-based dyes
    - clear tap water and water tinted with food coloring

For *drawing*, preschool and school-age children can

- use a variety of tools
    - water-based markers
    - crayons
    - chalk
    - pencils

- use an assortment of papers and other surfaces
    - manila
    - newsprint
    - butcher paper
    - grocery bags
    - computer paper
    - construction paper
    - oaktag (poster board)
    - tracing paper
    - paper plates
    - shelf paper
    - cardboard
    - STYROFOAM® trays.

For *modeling and molding,* preschool and school-age children can

- experiment with a variety of materials

  - homemade modeling doughs

  - doughs with amusing names and odd scientific properties
    - Silly Putty® [To make your own variation, combine 1 cup of white glue (such as Elmer's Glue-All®) with 1 cup of cornstarch.]
    - oobleck (also known as goobleck), which is an unstable substance that is a liquid and a solid at the same time (To make this fun concoction, place 1 cup of cornstarch in a bowl. Pour ½ cup of water over the mixture. Mix the ingredients well and let it sit until it hardens. When you pick it up, it will melt. Throw it in the air, and it will lose its shape and flatten like a pancake.)
    - slime [To make your own, mix 2 cups of white glue (such as Elmer's Glue-All®) in a bowl with several drops of food coloring. Slowly mix in 1 cup of liquid starch.]

- modeling (soft) clay

  - baking clay

  - plasticine (oil-based clay that never hardens)

- use a variety of tools

  - cookie cutters

  - board and hammer

  - mallet

  - melon baller

  - pizza cutter

  - masher and ricer

For *printing,* preschool and school-age children can

- use an assortment of papers
- experiment with a variety of tools

  - rubber stamps

  - sponges

  - dominoes

  - corks

  - golf balls

  - ink pads made by fastening a piece of firm foam rubber or a sponge shape onto a STYROFOAM® tray and then pouring tempera paint onto the foam or sponge

For *collages and assemblages*, preschool and school-age children can

- use a variety of small nontoxic items, including beads, bottle caps, cotton balls, doilies, fabric scraps, flowers, glitter, lace, shells, shoelaces, yarn, toothpicks, dried flowers, and marbles (Be careful about the size of materials that can be reached by children who might choke on them.)

- experiment with a variety of fasteners, including brads, binder clips, clothespins, rubber bands, staples, yarn, twine, twist ties, and paste

School-age children and preschool children with well-developed small-muscle skills might enjoy some of these special art activities:

- unique painting techniques
  - blow painting (using a straw to blow a glob of paint across paper)
  - spatter painting (using a toothbrush; screen; and stencils or items like leaves, flowers, and feathers)
  - crayon-resist painting (painting over crayon drawings with diluted paint)
  - folded painting (placing a glob of paint on a piece of paper, folding it, and then unfolding it)

- etching (using a fork, bottle cap, or empty ballpoint pen to etch a design on a printing "block" such as a STYROFOAM® food tray)

- puppetry
  - sock collage puppets (gluing collage materials that represent facial features onto a sock, glove, or lunch bag "head")
  - newspaper puppets (using rubber bands and rolled newspapers to form a puppet body that can be decorated and dressed)
  - papier-mâché puppets (dipping strips of newspaper into wallpaper paste, covering an inflated balloon, painting the hardened balloon to resemble a human or animal head, and sewing fabric around the painted head to give the puppet form)

- weaving (using chicken wire, berry containers, or mesh vegetable bags as weaving surfaces and using fingers, plastic needles, or a craft stick with a drilled hole to guide pipe cleaners, straws, yarn, ribbon, or floral wire in and out of the openings)

## Displaying Materials

Here are some ideas about storing art materials so they are accessible to children:

- Egg cartons with the edges taped together and holes pierced through the top can be used to hold scissors.

- Empty, round, gallon ice cream containers make good holders for paper and collage materials.

- A marker holder can be made by pouring plaster of Paris into a container and placing the markers upside-down in the plaster so that the closed ends of the caps are submerged in the plaster. When the plaster hardens, the caps will stay in the plaster, and the body of the markers can be removed from and returned to the caps.

- Empty, airtight margarine, butter, and cream cheese containers can be used to store clays and doughs.

- Clean yogurt containers with plastic lids make good glue or paste containers. So do squeezable mustard and ketchup bottles.

- Yarn, ribbon, or twine dispensers can be made from a cardboard box with dividers. The divided areas make convenient spaces for individual balls of materials, and they prevent tangling. Punch a hole in the top of the box over each space and draw the strands through the holes.

- Hang smocks on a pegboard with hooks.

While you will want to send most of the children's artwork home to their families, think about displaying some of it in your FCC home. This tells children that you value their efforts, ideas, and creations.

Invite children to decide which drawings, paintings, sculptures, collages, and mobiles they want to take home and which they would like to keep at your FCC home. When you hang their art, treat their creations as if they were museum pieces. Make sure each piece of artwork has the child's name and date. You can even frame their artwork by using construction paper, cardboard, craft sticks, colored rubber bands woven across cardboard, or inexpensive frames that you have picked up at a dollar store or yard sale.

# Caring and Teaching

Art is a form of creative expression, a way for children to convey what they know and feel and a way to understand other people's ideas and experiences. You play an important role in helping support children's efforts both to create and appreciate art.

In general, coloring books and adult-directed projects where everyone makes the same thing are not recommended for young children. Although they might keep children busy, these experiences do not encourage children to express themselves. Just as you want a child to feel free to paint a purple pumpkin, you want all children to create art that is truly theirs—not what an adult decides it should be.

## Responding to Each Child

In order to help children develop and learn through art, observe how they explore, experiment with, and use art materials. Offer them the kinds of open-ended materials listed in the previous section and watch what they create!

Young **infants** have experiences related to art when they watch the colors of sunlight refracted by a moving prism or when they feel fabrics and crumple papers of varying textures.

By the time infants are about a year old, you can give them large crayons, chalk, and playdough so they can begin to scribble and mold. Because mobile infants are still developing eye–hand coordination, their marks and scribbles appear to be random. Children may enjoy moving paintbrushes across paper, making lines. They may make circles with a crayon, filling up almost all of the white space on their papers.

When you interact with infants, you can help them learn by commenting on what they are doing.

| Observe | Reflect | Respond |
|---|---|---|
| The older children are sitting around the kitchen table, making collages and drawing with crayons. Jeremy, who is sitting in your lap, reaches into the basket of fabric samples. He pulls out a piece of velvet, brushes it against his cheek, and smiles. | Jeremy is curious about the art materials and is exploring the fabric samples by touching them. *(Objective 11, Demonstrates positive approaches to learning; Objective 26, Demonstrates knowledge of the physical properties of objects and materials)* | Comment on what Jeremy is doing and extend his experience. "You picked up the velvet, Jeremy. It feels soft, doesn't it? Let's see how other fabrics feel. Here is a piece of burlap. Let's rub it gently on your arm. It feels scratchy, doesn't it?" |

**Toddlers and twos** enjoy experimenting with drawing tools. It's almost as though they cannot wait to see what they can do next. A child may deliberately move his paintbrush in one direction and then suddenly try holding it at another angle. Children in these age-groups are not usually trying to represent anything specific; experimentation and control of the tools are becoming important to them.

Some 2-year-olds have enough fine motor control to use paste and scissors, so they enjoy making collages and assemblages. They may want to tear or cut magazine pages into small pieces that they paste onto colored construction paper.

| Observe | Reflect | Respond |
| --- | --- | --- |
| Jorge furrows his brow as he pastes the last piece of torn crepe paper onto a piece of construction paper. When he finishes, he looks at the wad of paste on top of his hand and shakes it back into the paste jar. Then he holds up his collage for you to admire. | Jorge is very involved in pasting and is determined to paste the entire pile of torn pieces on the construction paper. To remove the excess paste, he used a problem-solving strategy. *(Objective 11, Demonstrates positive approaches to learning)* | Describe what you see Jorge doing and encourage his pasting efforts: "Jorge, you pasted all of the pieces of crepe paper. Your collage is very interesting. I'll find some big buttons for you to paste on the paper if you'd like to add them tomorrow." |

**Preschool children** begin producing representational art. Houses, the sun, family members, and pets make frequent appearances in their artwork. Young preschoolers do not usually begin with a plan, but they often form a conclusion about what they drew, painted, or sculpted after they work for a little while (even if you cannot recognize their representations). Older preschoolers often plan their drawings and paintings. They take pride in their artistic accomplishments and want the adults in their lives to share their enthusiasm.

When you talk with preschool children about their art, help them reflect on their work. Describe what you see and ask open-ended questions that encourage children to think critically. Avoid making judgments and giving automatic praise like "That's pretty." Your goal is to help children understand the process of using art materials and become more skilled at representing their feelings and ideas.

| Observe | Reflect | Respond |
|---|---|---|
| As part of a study of butterflies, Keisha constructs a butterfly model with tissue paper and pipe cleaners. Then she asks for your help in hanging it from the ceiling. | Keisha's butterfly shows the characteristics of the monarch butterflies in the garden the group planted outdoors. *(Objective 25, Demonstrates knowledge of the characteristics of living things; Objective 33, Explores the visual arts)* | Ask questions that help Keisha think about her work, for example, "What do you want your butterfly to be able to do?...How did you decide what materials and colors to use?...What should we write to tell our visitors about your butterfly?" |

**School-age children** enjoy art projects they can work on and complete over time. They may spend several days perfecting a sketch, weaving, or sculpture. They also view art as a means of relaxation. They doodle and sketch in their notebooks to amuse themselves, or they might pound clay just for fun.

You can support school-age children's art experiences by asking about their interests and taking them to the library to check out books about favorite artists and art techniques. Provide older children with materials and space for working on projects. Support their work by asking open-ended questions and suggesting ways to extend their work.

| Observe | Reflect | Respond |
| --- | --- | --- |
| Tyrone has been spending hours after school every day, using photos from the Museum of Natural History as his guide for making polymer clay dinosaurs. | Tyrone is very proud of his dinosaur figures. I want to encourage his artistic efforts, but I'd like him to build on his interest in dinosaurs even more. | "Tyrone, do you remember the dinosaur exhibition you saw at the museum with your dad? Now that you've made so many dinosaurs, would like to make a diorama to show their environment? What do you think?" |

## Engaging Children of All Ages

While children often want to use art materials on their own, you will sometimes want to encourage them to undertake a group project. Here is an example.

Imagine that it is a pleasant afternoon in late spring. You and the children are just finishing a snack on a blanket in the backyard. The conversation has shifted to the puppet show the children are planning to perform for family night.

Nathan (3 years), Rosa (4 years), and Keisha (4 ½ years) have spent much of the last week making elaborate puppets for the show. They think that their preparations are complete, so they are confused when you ask them what they are planning to do about a backdrop.

Seeing the puzzled look on their faces, you explain what a backdrop is and discuss the benefits of having one. Then you suggest that the whole group help paint one for the puppet theater, and you remind them that you have a good supply of butcher paper.

"What will we use to color our backdrop?" asks Keisha.

"Color. Color," says Tamika (19 months).

"Yes, *color*," you repeat. "Nathan, will you say *color*, too?"

You and Nathan repeat the word *color* so many times, you both start laughing.

"Quiero usar los crayones", says Rosa.

You respond, "Oh, you do? Does everyone agree that we should use crayons?"

After the children chorus, "Yes," Keisha says, "I'll get them." Tyrone (age 8), who has been listening, offers to help her bring out the butcher paper, scissors, and the basket of crayons. When they return, you ask the children to help you lay out the paper on the patio and hold down the corners with large stones.

Keisha, Rosa, Nathan, Jorge (2 ½ years), and Tamika scurry around the paper to join Tyrone. They are ready to start coloring. Holding Jeremy in your arms, you join the children and give Jeremy a crayon to hold.

As the children draw, Keisha becomes concerned that the younger children are ruining the project. After discussing alternatives, the older children decide to make a collage for the backdrop. That way, it won't matter if it contains scribbles. Everyone except Jeremy goes to look for things in the yard that can be used for the collage.

After commenting on the treasures the children collected, you ask, "How can you get these things to stick to the butcher paper?"

"Goma en barra", Rosa suggests.

"The glue sticks! That's a great idea," you agree. "Let's bring out some paste, too, because Jorge is the Paste King!"

Tyrone, who understands that you need to watch the younger children, runs inside with Rosa to get the glue and paste. When the other children resume their work on the backdrop, Jeremy claps and coos from his observation post in your lap.

By showtime, Jeremy, Tamika, and Jorge may have pretty much forgotten about their coloring and gluing experience. For them, exploring the materials was more important than using the collage later for the puppet show. However, Tyrone, Nathan, Rosa, and Keisha take great pride in pointing out the backdrop to their families.

This scenario illustrates a number of important points:

- Working together on a project offers children opportunities to solve problems, develop social skills, and share an experience that fosters a sense of community.

- Art processes matter most to young children, even when finalizing a product.

- Art experiences foster meaningful conversations and vocabulary development, and they are opportunities for helping dual-language learners practice English.

- When children are at different stages in their development of art skills, accommodations are necessary.

- Outdoor art experiences differ from indoor art experiences.

- Art is exciting!

# Partnering With Families

Many families think of art as drawings and other products they can put on their refrigerators. Because it involves much more than that, it is important to share with them the great value of art as a way for children to express their ideas and feelings. You can help families understand what their children are doing as they explore art materials and how art experiences promote children's learning and development. Try the following *LearningGames®* activities in your program and share them with families. You can also share information by sending the letter to families about art.

## *LearningGames®* for Art

Birth–12 months

### Game 31, "First Crayons"

Playing with crayons and paper introduces babies to tools for drawing and writing. Encourage the family to give their child a crayon and paper and to talk about the crayon and any marks the child makes. Remind the family that their baby explores objects in many ways. The child may feel it, look at it, and even taste it, so it's important to watch the baby while he or she is exploring the crayon. When you send home a child's "drawing," explain that you use similar techniques in your program.

12–24 months

### Game 62, "Painting With Water"

This game is fun to play with children outdoors. A half-filled bucket of water and a sponge are the only things needed to get started. The child dips the sponge; squeezes it out a little; and begins to sponge the trees, steps, walls, or rocks. The game may also be played indoors on the kitchen floor with a bowl of water, a paintbrush, and some toys or plastic dishes to "paint." Invite families to take photos of the activity to share with you.

24–36 months

### Game 95, "Cut and Paste"

Cutting with scissors is a great way to have fun while children learn to use their wrists and hands. Learning to cut with scissors takes time and practice. Encourage families to use safe, children's scissors and to start by having their children make small cuts in a strip of paper or snip around the edge of a larger sheet. The fun can be extended by pasting the cut scraps of paper onto a large piece of paper.

36–48 months

### Game 123, "Painting With My Hands"

Finger painting is a fun, sensory art experience for children. Are families concerned about the mess? Show them what you do: Protect clothing with a smock, cover the table with a plastic shower curtain, and have children paint on a cookie sheet. Using a single color at a time helps children see how the paint moves as they move their arms and hands. They will also delight in mixing two colors, seeing, for example, that red and yellow make orange and that blue and yellow make green. Save each creation by pressing a sheet of newsprint on top of it.

48–60 months

### Game 168, "Build a Person"

Playing with dough is a great way to increase children's finger skills. This game supports fine motor development while increasing children's awareness of their bodies. Provide materials such as craft sticks for legs and arms, and buttons for eyes and noses. Explain to families how and why you often make playdough with the children.

# A Letter to Families About Art

Dear Families,

Art is an important part of my program. I provide children with a variety of art experiences every day. Drawing, painting, pasting, molding, and constructing are enjoyable, and they provide very important opportunities for learning. As they explore art materials, children express their ideas and feelings, improve their eye–hand coordination, learn to name colors and describe textures, and feel proud of their creative efforts.

While children are engaged in art activities, I talk with them about what they are doing. I ask questions that encourage them to think about their ideas, express their feelings, and experiment with the tools and materials.

The children and I are primarily interested in creative processes. I support your child's confidence by saying such things as "Tell me about your picture," instead of asking something like "Is that a house?" Think how a child would feel if his picture weren't one of a house!

Here are some ideas for exploring art with your child at home:

Children love to bring their artwork home to share with you. Take time to talk with your child about his or her art. Comment on the colors and the different lines, shapes, and patterns. Here are some questions you might ask your child:

- How did you get the pieces of crepe paper to stick to the construction paper?
- How did you decide what colors to use in your painting?
- What do you like best about your sculpture?
- Where should we hang your mobile so that we can all enjoy it?

You can also help your child appreciate other artwork. When you look at books together, talk about the illustrations with your child. Discuss the art in your home, too.

Your child can explore art in almost any room. You might designate a kitchen or living room drawer as an art drawer, or you might use a bookshelf or sturdy cardboard box. Include crayons; water-based markers; paper; a pair of child-sized, blunt-edged scissors; glue; and a container with a variety of collage materials. Children don't need coloring books. With their own imaginations and your support, their artistic talents will flourish.

Sincerely,

# Toys and Games

**13**

# Toys and Games

Nathan (3 years) is sitting at the table with a basket of pegs and a pegboard. He places a peg in each hole until they are all filled. When he is finished, he looks up at you and starts to sing, "Hap' birfday to me."

You say, "You made a birthday cake with your pegs," and join him in singing the full song. Turning to Rosa (4 years), you notice that she has is selecting her pegs more carefully, making a full row of each color. She stops, noticing that there are no other colors. "You made rows of red, yellow, blue, green, and purple," you say pointing to each row. "There aren't any other colors! What will you use now?" Rosa looks at her pegboard, selects red pegs, and fills the next row. Then she fills solid rows of yellow, blue, green, and purple. You write an observation note about how each child used the pegs in very different ways, each learning something from the experience.

The best toys for children are durable and safe, and they can be used creatively by children of different ages and abilities. They include anything that children can explore, put together, pull apart, push and pull, stack, string, or construct. Some toys are designed to entertain children and capture their attention, such as mobiles that swing and play music, and balls with colorful designs. Other toys are structured to fit together in a particular way: puzzles, nesting cups, pegboards, and stacking rings. Still others are open-ended and can be used in a variety of ways: to build and stack, or to create a pattern or design. There are also board games that must be played according to rules children have to learn and follow.

Effective toys capture children's attention, keep them engaged, and help them acquire and strengthen new skills. Children develop small-muscle skills and eye–hand coordination as they grasp, pull apart, fit together, fill and dump, stack, string, or construct with interlocking blocks. When they complete a task successfully with self-correcting toys such as puzzles or shape sorters, they gain confidence in their abilities. Playing games with others and working together on tasks teaches important social skills. Children learn how objects can be used by exploring the toys you provide. They learn that a rattle will make a noise only if they shake it and that a round block will only fit through a round hole, not a square one, if the hole is the same size as the block. They practice math skills as they match, make patterns, group, and compare objects.

# Setting Up for Toys and Games

To enable children to use toys and games safely and constructively, consider what is appropriate for each age, where children will play, and how you will store the toys so children can find them and return them when they are finished.

---

**Keeping Children Safe and Healthy**

For the youngest children, select toys that are washable and made of nontoxic materials. Avoid toys that have the following characteristics:

- Breakable parts, sharp or jagged edges, or exposed nails, wires, pins, or splinters
- Small pieces (smaller than 1 ½ inches in diameter) that can become lodged in noses, ears, throats, or windpipes
- Cords and strings that could become wound around a child's neck
- Parts that could pinch, pierce, or trap children's hair or clothing

For up-to-date information about toy safety, go to the U.S. Consumer Product Safety Commission Web site: http://www.cpsc.gov.

---

## Choosing Toys and Games

In selecting toys for your program, you want to get the most for your investment. Good advice comes from TRUCE (Teachers Resisting Unhealthy Children's Entertainment). Their Web site (www.truceteachers.org) is an excellent resource for information about appropriate toys and for learning about recalls. They recommend buying toys that

- can be used in many ways
- enable children to be in charge of their play
- appeal to children at more than one age
- are not linked to video games, television shows, or movies
- promote respectful, nonstereotypical, nonviolent interactions
- help children develop skills and further their learning

Keep in mind that some of the most interesting toys for young children are often ones you do not have to buy. They are simply common objects and natural materials that can be explored safely. Plastic containers, cardboard boxes, crinkly tissue paper, wooden and plastic kitchen utensils, pots and pans, leaves, and shells appeal to young children as much as many toys you can purchase (and sometimes even more). The ages, developmental abilities, and individual interests of children are important considerations in selecting toys and games for your program.

**Infants, toddlers, and twos** need toys that are safe to touch, mouth, smell, look at, listen to, ride on, manipulate, and toss. Here are some suggestions:

- mobiles with patterns, circles, and high contrast, and those that make music

- unbreakable mirrors placed on the wall near the floor

- stuffed animals and dolls and some made of rubber, plastic, and wood

- small rattles, plastic keys, teething rings, measuring spoons

- balls of all types: clutch balls with easily grasped, indented surfaces; balls with chimes or visible objects rolling inside; and balls that roll in unpredictable ways, such as weighted balls and oddly shaped ones

- stacking rings, nesting cups, foam boards, shape sorters

- busy boxes and surprise boxes that pop up

- push-and-pull toys, such as carriages and child-sized shopping carts for children who are just beginning to walk; play lawn mower; wagons for sturdier toddlers and twos

- ride-on toys

- simple puzzles with 4–5 pieces for toddlers and puzzles with 6–12 pieces for twos

- pegboards with large pegs, stacking rings (with 5–10 pieces), Bristle Blocks®, large DUPLO® pieces, large plastic snap beads, plastic nuts and bolts, shape sorters

- plastic, wooden, and metal cars, trucks, buses, trains, and airplanes, including some with movable parts (for example, steering wheels that turn; bulldozer shovels that pick up and dump; cherry pickers that they can raise and lower; and knobs, levers, buttons, and wheels of all sorts)

- tunnels or large cardboard boxes through which children can crawl

**Preschool and school-age children** have more refined finger control. They can sort and match, create designs and constructions, and play board games that involve taking turns with other children. Here are the types of toys to consider for this age-group:

- wooden and cardboard puzzles that range from 12-piece puzzles to 50-piece jigsaw puzzles, and puzzles with 100 pieces or more for older children.

- colored cubes, pegboards, mosaic blocks and tiles, parquetry blocks, smaller beads and laces for stringing, magnetic boards with shapes for making patterns and designs

- collections to sort, match, and compare, such as plastic bottle caps, buttons, keys, shells, seeds, small plastic animals and vehicles, plastic fasteners (for example, from bread bags)

- construction toys such as LEGO® pieces, Unifix® cubes, and geoboards

- matching games, dominoes, card games (for example, fish, concentration, hearts, gin rummy), and simple board games like "Candy Land®," bingo, "Boggle®," "Sorry®," "Uno®," "Chutes and Ladders®," checkers, Chinese checkers, chess, junior scrabble, mancala, and parcheesi

- dollhouse, furniture, and small dolls

- model farm buildings, fences, animals, and people

### Simple Modifications for Children With Disabilities[1]

- Glue knobs or corks to puzzles pieces, and add foam curlers to build up the handles of spoons, brushes, crayons, and markers for children with limited fine motor skills.

- Hang toys securely on a sturdy frame so children with motor impairments can reach them and not worry about dropping them. The frames can be placed on the floor, attached to a table, or attached to a wheelchair or stander.

- Attach toys to a firm surface (such as foam core, pegboard, or indoor–outdoor carpet) with Velcro®, string, or elastic.

- Select toys with large pieces (such as puzzles) and simplify games and toys.

- Invite the child's physical or occupational therapist to visit your program and suggest ways to adapt your space and toys to meet the child's unique abilities.

The Toy Industry Foundation publishes a resource entitled "Let's Play: A Guide to Toys for Children with Special Needs." It lists toys that all children, with and without disabilities, can use successfully. You can find it by logging on to www.toyindustryfoundation.org.

## Displaying Toys and Games

Toys and games can be used on a table or on the floor. If toys are stored on the bottom shelf of a bookcase or room divider, children can get them when they want to play with them. Avoid using toy chests. They are safety hazards, and it is difficult for children to find toys in them.

Group similar toys together. This helps children locate their favorite puzzles, transportation toys, push-and-pull toys, and so forth. Grouping by type also helps children learn to classify objects.

Put out a manageable selection of toys. Too many toys can overwhelm children, and too few can lead to arguments and unhappy feelings. Try to provide duplicates of popular toys to minimize conflicts. Rotate toys regularly. When you bring out a familiar item again, children's interest may be renewed.

# Caring and Teaching

When children have access to high-quality toys, they experiment, explore, build, discover, and create for hours. By observing purposefully, taking a real interest in what they do, and responding to them, you will learn what interests each child and be able to appreciate what each child is doing and learning.

## Responding to Each Child

As you watch children play with toys and games, notice whether a child

- selects and cares for materials independently or only with your help
- explores the physical properties of the materials (functional play), builds and creates (constructive play), engages in pretend play, or follows the rules of a game
- is developing small-muscle skills and eye–hand coordination
- uses logical thinking skills to work with materials (e.g., sorting and classifying, patterning, measuring, comparing, counting)

For very young **infants**, you are the best toy! Infants prefer watching your face, hearing your voice, and being held more than they like any toy. Once they can focus their vision better and hold things in their fists, they put everything in their mouths. When they can sit up, a favorite activity is dumping and filling. Place a basket of toys or other safe items nearby, and infants will proceed to pull out every object they can reach, dropping each on the floor and then reaching for another. They also enjoy tossing and rolling, so you want to give them plenty of space and soft, unbreakable toys and balls.

Just as an infant lets you know when he is hungry, tired, or in need of changing, his behavior lets you know when he is ready to play or when he is finished with one play experience and ready for another.

| Observe | Reflect | Respond |
| --- | --- | --- |
| Jeremy lies on his tummy on a mat. He reaches for the plastic keys and brings them to his mouth. He watches Tamika push a red plastic truck across the rug and smiles. Then he scoots along the floor on his stomach in her direction, trying to get to where she is and reaching for the truck. | Jeremy is using his whole hand to grasp objects. *(Objective 7, Demonstrates fine motor strength and coordination)*<br><br>He is beginning to move purposefully. *(Objective 4, Demonstrates traveling skills)*<br><br>He watches and responds to other children. *(Objective 2, Establishes and sustains positive relationships)* | Talk about what Jeremy is doing: "You like chewing on those keys, don't you? They are smooth and hard. Now you are moving across the room all by yourself!"<br><br>Encourage Jeremy's interest in other toys and children: "You see Tamika playing with that red truck. I bet you want to play with it, too. We don't have another red truck, but here's a red car for Jeremy to play with. You can push your car just like Tamika." |

**Toddlers and twos** are fascinated by toys. As long as you do not give them too many choices and you show an interest in what they are doing, their play can be creative and joyful. Engage children in conversation about what they want to play with and what they intend to do. As they develop expressive language, use open-ended questions to encourage them to think and talk about what they are doing.

| Observe | Reflect | Respond |
| --- | --- | --- |
| Jorge is working on a new 5-piece puzzle of farm animals. He fits two pieces in place and then tries to fit the others. He tries one piece, then another, then a third, but none of them fits. He tries them again and gets one to fit. Then he looks at you and asks, "He'p?" | Jorge stayed with this task even though he was having difficulty. *(Objective 11, Demonstrates positive approaches to learning)*<br><br>He is able to ask for help. *(Objective 9, Uses spoken language to express thoughts and needs; Objective 38, Demonstrates progress in speaking English)* | Point out what he has accomplished: "That's a new puzzle, and you put three pieces in the right places!"<br><br>Encourage his perseverance: "Some of those pieces are hard to fit, but you didn't give up."<br><br>Provide the right amount of support: "Let's look at these two pieces and turn them around a little. Does that help you see where they go?" |

**Preschool children** can use toys quite independently and enjoy the challenge of putting together a new puzzle, creating and stringing a pattern with beads, or make a design with colorful table blocks. Careful observation will give you ideas about what to say and how to encourage their play. By talking with them, you show how much you value what they are doing.

| Observe | Reflect | Respond |
|---|---|---|
| Rosa and Keisha are playing with Unifix® cubes. Each has made a long line of cubes so that, when they hold them up, their constructions bend over. Keisha says, "Mine is taller than yours." Rosa responds, "Muy grande". | Rosa and Keisha are playing together. *(Objective 2, Establishes and sustains positive relationships)*<br><br>They are comparing their constructions. *(Objective 22, Compares and measures)* | Share your interest in what they are doing: "You each made a very long line of Unifix® cubes."<br><br>Make a suggestion: "Let's put them flat on the table to see how long they are. Then we can count them together." |

**School-age children** enjoy open-ended materials with which they can create patterns, designs, and constructions. Remember that they like to work on projects over time. If you can provide a protected place for them to work on and store a jigsaw puzzle, they can come back to it whenever they wish. School-age children also like board and card games they can play with you or with other children. Even as they get older, children want to know that you notice and take an interest in what they are doing and thinking.

| Observe | Reflect | Respond |
|---|---|---|
| Tyrone finishes his homework and gets out a deck of cards. "Let's play gin," he says. "I've been playing with my Dad, and I'm getting really good. I bet I can beat you." | Tyrone is confident about his gin rummy skills, and we have fun together. I don't want to discourage Tyrone, but Jeremy's cold is making him very cranky and the other children also need my attention.<br><br>What interesting challenge can I offer Tyrone while he waits for me to play with him? | Explain, "I'd love to play, Tyrone, but I can't until some of the other children go home. Meanwhile, let me show you how you can play solitaire on the computer. I think you will really like the program." |

## Engaging Children of All Ages

It often feels like a juggling act, keeping a group of children who range in age from a few months to many years happily engaged with toys and games. However, it can be done! Here's an example of what might happen.

On the floor, you place the three stacking toys you recently purchased at a yard sale. Sitting with Jeremy, you wait to see how long it takes the other children to find the new toys. You don't have to wait long. Jorge (2 ½ years), Tamika (19 months), Rosa (4 years), and Tyrone (8 years) all come over.

"Look at these brightly colored rings," you say. You hand one to Jeremy, who puts it in his mouth and then bangs it on the floor. Tamika reaches for two rings from the same toy and bangs them together. Rosa and Jorge take over the two remaining stacking ring sets, dump them, and proceed to stack and restack the rings.

"I know what I can do with these," announces Tyrone. "I can spin them. My dad used to do that for me when I was little. Watch this." He takes two rings and spins them on the floor. They delight all of the children.

The play continues for a few more minutes, but you realize that Rosa and Nathan are beginning to lose interest. You ask, "What else do you think you can do with these rings?"

"We could squash them with our feet," offers Tyrone. Nathan gets a ring and stands on it.

"Is that taking good care of our toys?" you ask.

"No. I was only kidding," responds Tyrone.

Rosa takes one and puts it on her head. "Hat," she says as she balances it on her head. Nathan takes one and puts it on his head. They both laugh.

"Cook food. Baby," suggests Nathan, and he and Rosa take some rings to the house corner you set up. They begin to pretend to cook.

"Tyrone, why don't you and I play a board game while I keep Jeremy and Tamika busy on the rug? You pick one." Tyrone runs to get his favorite game. While he sets up the pieces, you get Tamika and Jeremy started with a few other toys you know they will enjoy.

During the game, you talk to Jeremy and Tamika about what they are doing. "I see you put a red ring on the post, Tamika. Can you find one that will fit on top? Jeremy, you like squeezing that ball. It's very soft." Tamika wanders off to get another toy, and everyone remains occupied for the next 15 minutes. That is long enough for you and Tyrone almost to finish the game.

"We'll finish this game when the other children are napping," you tell Tyrone, and he helps you put it on a high shelf. "It's time to clean up and get ready to go outside now."

Here are some things to keep in mind to ensure that children of all ages in your family child care home can enjoy using toys and games at the same time.

- The same toys can be used with equal pleasure by children of different ages if they are open-ended and safe.
- Your involvement in children's play is very important.
- You do not have to involve all of the children in the same activity at one time.
- Children can make up their own ways of using toys, as long as they are not destructive.

## Partnering With Families

Toys and games, whether purchased, collected, or made with common household objects, are wonderful learning materials for young children. The first and most important criteria are that anything you give children must be safe and age appropriate. Just as toys and games are essential materials for a family child care home, children need to have play materials at home as well. The *LearningGames*® related to this topic show families how simple and easy-to-make toys can support children's learning. Sending the letter about toys and games is another way to share information with families.

### *LearningGames*® for Toys and Games

Birth–12 months

**Game 12, "Watching a Toy Go Out of Sight"**

Seeing a toy disappear and reappear will delight a baby and help the baby learn that things still exist even when they are out of sight. That concept is known as *object permanence*. This game is playing "Peek-a-Boo" (*LearningGames* activity 9*)* with a toy. Later, families can play "Hiding and Finding" (*LearningGames* activity 21*)*.

12–24 months

### Game 50, "Nesting Objects"

Many *LearningGames* activities can be played with simple materials found in the kitchen. This is one of those games. It is played with simple household containers of graduated sizes, such as juice cans, measuring cups, or plastic storage dishes. As a baby explores these objects, she may discover that the little one fits inside the big one. What a surprise! Putting things in order and understanding size prepare children for certain kinds of later math learning.

24–36 months

### Game 77, "Color Sorting"

Use and share this *LearningGames* activities to help children learn the important skill of sorting. Point out how younger 2-year-olds enjoy putting the red blocks in one place and the blue blocks in another.

36–48 months

### Game 130, "Matching Among Similar Pictures"

Remind families that when their children were 2 years old they used a *LearningGames* activity called "Pair and Sort Pictures." In that game, their children found two pictures that were alike. Explain that at this age children can look at four (or more) similar pictures and find two that are exactly alike. They can spy with their little eyes! Show families the version of this game that you use in your program.

48–60 months

### Game 160, "Move Up Five"

This is a simple board game you can make for your program and that families can make and play with their children. Players take turns picking cards with one, two, three, four, or five dots. Then they move that number of spaces around a homemade game board. Children practice counting and learn that each number stands for a particular quantity.

---

[1] Assistive Technology Training Project Staff (1996). *Infusing assistive technology into early childhood classrooms* (draft version). Phoenix, AZ: Author.

# A Letter to Families About Toys and Games

Dear Families,

You will see a wide variety of toys and games in my family child care home. Some are purchased, and some are homemade. Almost anything that children can explore, put together, pull apart, push and pull, stack, string, or construct is a toy. Toys are designed for children's enjoyment. They are also wonderful tools for learning.

Babies like toys they can feel, look at, taste, smell, and shake. They learn that a rattle will make a noise only if it is moved and that a round block will only fit through a round hole, not a square one, if the hole is the same size as the block. Toddlers and twos like to push wagons, use busy boxes, pile blocks into containers and dump them out, build a tower, knock it down, and then build it again. The preschool children in my program handle puzzles, construct designs with blocks, sort and classify objects, and follow the rules for simple board games. They practice math skills as they match, make patterns, group, and compare objects. The school-age children enjoy using construction toys to create designs and structures, and they like to play board games.

As children play, I talk with them to teach new words, engage them in conversation, and challenge them to test new ideas. I might say:

"I see you used all the triangles and diamonds to make your design."

"You put the buttons in different piles. How did you decide where to put each button?"

Here are some ideas that can help your child get the most from playing with toys and games at home:

**Common household objects make wonderful toys.** Some of the best toys are not commercial products; they are simply common household objects. An empty box; large empty thread spools; pots and pans; plastic food containers; kitchen utensils; and collections of buttons, bottle caps, keys, seeds, shells, and rocks are just a few of the things that children use as toys.

**A few good toys are better than too many.** Too many toys can overwhelm a young child. It's far better to have a few good toys that can be used in a variety of ways. Look for toys that encourage children to be active and that are sturdy and safe.

**Keep in mind that you are your child's favorite toy.** No toy can replace the joy your child experiences by having you as a playmate! Your interest and involvement make playing with toys even more fun and engaging.

Sincerely,

# Stories and Books

# Stories and Books

Nathan (3 years) is sitting on the couch, looking at the picture book you made together about his family. You say to him, "You miss your Mommy, Nathan. May I look at the pictures with you?" He nods his head, and you join him on the couch. He looks at the pictures and names each family member. You describe what is happening in each picture, "This was the day you went to the zoo with your grandma. Here you are again, playing in the snow!"

When you have looked at the pictures twice, Nathan goes to the bookshelf and brings you the book *Are You My Mommy?* As you sit together to read it, Jorge (2 ½ years) and Rosa (4 years) join you on the couch.

Sharing stories and books with children can be among the most treasured times of your day. Holding a child in your lap while one or two others snuggle next to you gives the children and you a chance to relax, talk, look at illustrations, and enjoy a shared experience. Books open the world to children. Through pictures and stories, children clarify ideas and feelings. They hear about people who are just like them and people who are different. They are introduced to new ideas, places, and language. Books can soothe an upset child, make a child laugh, and excite a child's imagination.

Your interaction as you cuddle with a book, your enthusiasm, the way you bring a story to life through your dramatic reading, and your interesting questions make the experience special for children. When you know the children in your group well, you can choose wonderful books for an infant to manipulate and explore, for a toddler or 2-year-old who is about to acquire a new sister or brother, and for a preschool child who is fascinated by dinosaurs. You can also help a school-age child find a copy of the book on which a favorite movie was based, such as *The Lion, the Witch, and the Wardrobe* or other titles in the *Chronicles of Narnia* series.

Books also play a major role in helping children become lifelong readers. Children who are used to being around books when they are young are likely to become good readers when they get to school. Loving books is a powerful incentive for children to learn to read.

# Setting Up for Stories and Books

## Choosing Books

Select high-quality books that you will enjoy sharing with the children. Keep the children's developmental abilities in mind and look for books that respect diversity and promote inclusion. Rotate and add new books to encourage children's interests, but keep old favorites available for repeated (and repeated and repeated) readings. Offer books in children's home languages as well as in English.

Include some homemade books. Young children love books with pictures and stories about themselves. You can get out a book with family pictures when a child feels sad about saying good-bye to a parent. You can help children remember the first snowy day by sharing a book with pictures of them when they were frolicking in the snow and building a snowman. Digital cameras are a wonderful tool for making books.

Once you've picked out books for your family child care home, look at the collection as a whole. Do you want to change it in any way? The National Association for Family Child Care accreditation standards require providers to have at least 10 age-appropriate books each for child.[1] Keep the following criteria in mind as you select books:

- Do they address a variety of topics?
- Do they show people of all ages, differing abilities, various ethnicities, and different economic classes in respectful ways?
- Do men and women (boys and girls) take on a variety of roles?
- Does your collection include both fiction and nonfiction?
- Do you have books in a variety of sizes and shapes, from board books to big books?

You can keep your collection fresh and interesting by borrowing books from your local library. Yard sales and thrift stores are good sources of inexpensive books to expand your collection and replace worn books. Subscriptions to magazines, such as *Cricket, Ranger Rick*, or *My Big Backyard, Sports Illustrated for Kids, National Geographic Kids*, or *Muse*, will encourage children to look forward to new and interesting reading material each month.

Wear and tear on books cannot be avoided when young children handle them. Do not let that stop you from offering books to them. Although you expect wear and tear, always model the way to handle books carefully. Only display books that are in good repair. Torn books give the message that it is all right to tear books. Books in good condition show that books are taken care of well in your FCC home. Repair torn books before returning them to the bookshelf. Preschool and school-age children can help repair books.

## Displaying Books and Props

Children can look at books and read at almost any time, in any room of your house or in a book nook area that you set up specially. A cozy area that offers both physical and emotional comfort can make looking at books one of the children's favorite experiences in your FCC program. The key to helping children love books is to make their use inviting.

Whether using shared or separate space for your program, the following suggestions will help you set up a place for stories and books:

**Locate books in a quiet place** away from traffic and with soft, comfortable places to sit or recline. Sofas, armchairs, and glider rockers are inviting places for children to look at books by themselves, with a friend, or with you.

**Make sure the area is well lit.** Natural light is always best. Add a standing lamp, table lamp, or ceiling fixture if additional light is needed.

**Add softness** by providing overstuffed floor cushions, a covered mattress, stuffed animals, and dolls. A carpet or rug enables children to stretch out comfortably on the floor with a book. Beanbag chairs are great places for older children to settle, but they should not be used if you have children under age 3 in your program because they present a safety hazard.

**Locate electrical equipment close to electrical outlets and with cords safely out of children's reach.** This includes such items as lamps and CD players.

**Furnish the area with a bookshelf** on which to display books. You might want to include a stand for big books.

**Store books on low shelves** that children can reach easily. If a bookcase is not available, try hanging some shelves in a closet.

**Display books for infants, toddlers, twos, and preschool children in a standing position with the covers facing out.** Because young children cannot yet read titles, it is easier for them to identify books by their front covers. If you do not have space to display books that way, store them loosely on low shelves so that children can flip through them and see the covers easily.

**Add more books as children develop book-handling skills.** If you have several children who have not developed book-handling skills yet, put out just a few books at first but offer at least two books per child.

**Include books for children throughout your family child care home.** For instance, put a basket of books about cars or buildings near the block area and put books about food and nutrition in the kitchen and the dramatic play area.

**Enrich your library area with literacy-related materials and props.** Include materials for story retelling, listening, and writing. For example, flannel boards, story-related objects, clothesline story props, and puppets encourage children to retell stories they have heard. Set up a listening area with headphones and a cassette or CD player so children can listen to their favorite books on tape while following the pictures and turning the pages of the books. A writing area can include a shelf for materials and a table and chairs for writing. Include props such as alphabet strips, name cards, a variety of papers and writing tools, letter stamps, stencils, a stapler, and a hole punch.

Remember that books and other print materials should be used in many different ways. For example, to inspire twos and preschoolers to use blocks in new ways, you might share books like *Changes, Changes* by Pat Hutchins; *Build It Up and Knock It Down* by Tom Hunter; and *Block City*, in which Daniel Kirk illustrates a poem by Robert Louis Stevenson. David Macaulay's books, such as *City, Unbuilding,* and *Building Big* will inspire school-age children's block play. Magazines, calendars, and catalogs are interesting materials for dramatic play. In fact, you can find books to place in all of the experience areas of your FCC program. See *Literacy: The Creative Curriculum Approach* for good books to include for dramatic play, toys and games, art, sand and water, discovery, music and movement, cooking, computers, and outdoors—and more books for blocks.

# Caring and Teaching

Children's positive relationships with you enhance their enjoyment of stories and books. Exploring books and telling stories should be a daily experience and can be a way to calm an upset child. Make sure you read to every child, every day, either individually or in a small group. Reading aloud is one of the best ways to help children become successful readers. Don't assume that children who know how to read no longer want adults to read to them. Listening to a book being read aloud is a pleasure at all ages. Children will look forward to the next chapter in a classic book, such as *Misty of Chincoteague*, or the latest book by a popular living author such as Phyllis Reynolds Naylor.

Here are some general tips for reading and storytelling with young children:

**Become familiar with the book before you read it to children.** Think about what words might be new to the children so you can explain them. Also think of questions you might ask about the pictures or the text to help them understand the story.

**Tell stories as well as read them.** The first time you read a story to a very young child, you might want to tell the story in your own words instead of reading it as it was written. You can also tell stories by using wordless books and other storytelling props.

**Make reading interactive.** Set the stage. Snuggle. Build anticipation and excitement. Read dramatically, such as by pitching your voice high for Mama Bear and low for Papa Bear. Involve children in telling the story. Comment and wait for children to respond. Ask questions, give children enough time to answer, and offer prompts if necessary. Encourage children to chant a book's refrain or fill in a missing rhyme. When the story has ended, ask whether they liked the story and whether they want to hear it again.

**Follow the children's lead.** Be ready to stop when the children lose interest. Do not require children to sit still during story time.

**Be prepared to read the same story again and again.** Children have favorites and do not tire of hearing those stories every day.

**Link books to the daily routines and events in the children's lives.** If you're having difficulty calming a child for a nap, you might say goodnight to some of the objects in the room, just as in Margaret Wise Brown's *Goodnight Moon*. Sometimes you might say goodnight as the characters do in *Good Night, Gorilla*.

**Select books that children are able to connect with their firsthand experiences.** Is a child having a bad day? So is Alexander in *Alexander and the Terrible, Horrible, No Good, Very Bad Day.* There are books for every event in a child's life: a new baby, a new pet, a new home, and a new school. Mollie Bang's *When Sophie Gets Angry, Really, Really Angry* will intrigue an angry child. A child who is upset because her "blankie" was misplaced will be comforted by Mo Willem's *Knuffle Bunny* or Leslie Patricelli's *Blankie.* Older siblings will identify with Lilly's feelings about newborn baby Julius in Kevin Hanke's *Julius, the Baby of the World.*

**Take advantage of storytelling and reading opportunities as they occur.** Respond when, for example, a child brings you a book to read, comes to listen to a book while you are reading to another child, or settles down under the tree in your play yard. Storytelling and book reading can happen anywhere, and you can read a book to just one child as well as to a small group.

**Extend children's learning.** For example, *Build It Up and Knock It Down*, a book by Tom Hunter, is based on the song of the same name. Once you have read the book, you can listen to the song on a compact disc, and the older children can sing along. They can act it out, play an opposites game, build and knock down block structures, and crawl in and out of large boxes. The book *Market Days*, by Louise Ehlert, could lead to a trip to a market, making collages, and using vegetable props for dramatic play.

**Make your own books.** Children of all ages love homemade books, especially when the books are about them. Digital cameras are wonderful for making illustrations. You can create picture books by pasting photographs or magazine pictures to cardboard and then covering them with clear sticky paper. Bind the books with string or yarn threaded through holes in the margin. Make indestructible cloth books by drawing illustrations of everyday objects on muslin with permanent markers or nontoxic fabric paint. Help the children make books about themselves by using photographs. Ask the children to talk about each picture, and write down what they say. Write books with children about their experiences in family child care.

# Responding to Each Child

**Infants** explore books with their hands, mouths, noses, and toes as well as their eyes. For very young children, book experiences are sometimes book chewing, shaking, banging, sniffing, and looking. They enjoy exploring books that have parts to move and feel, such as tabs, flaps, holes, and a variety of textures. They want to listen to stories and look at books if they can sit on your lap and snuggle with you. Choose a time when the baby is alert and well-rested. Find a comfortable position for both you and the baby, perhaps with the baby in your lap or lying on the floor next to you. Read only a couple of pages and let the child turn the pages if he or she can. Read the baby's favorites again and again.

Older infants begin to recognize and point to pictures. They like simple, bold illustrations. As they grow older, they are interested in pictures of familiar objects such as food, toys, and pets. They also enjoy pictures of babies, families, and everyday experiences. They can sit and listen for longer periods as you read very simple stories. However, to keep the reading experience fun and exciting for the child, be prepared to stop at any point and start again when the child is ready.

Here are some tips for reading books with infants:

**Provide sturdy books** made of thick cardboard, soft vinyl, or washable cloth. Include books with pages that are easy to turn, such as hinged books with stiff pages. Choose books with one or two illustrations per page and with simple language or no words at all.

**Offer a toy** for a child to hold and chew while you read. For example, hand her a bear and explain, "Here's a cuddly bear. It's like the bear in the book."

**Focus the child's attention** by pointing to and naming things in the picture, for example, " There's the baby's nose. Here's your nose."

**Take cues** from the child's gestures, sounds, or words. For example, respond, "Yes, that's a baby, just like you!" or "You're pointing to the dump truck. You like big trucks."

| Observe | Reflect | Respond |
|---|---|---|
| Jeremy is snuggled on your lap, looking at the board book version of *Brown Bear, Brown Bear, What Do You See?* He pats the book as you read several pages. | Jeremy likes to explore books by touching and looking at them. *(Objective 11, Demonstrates positive approaches to learning; Objective 26, Demonstrates knowledge of the physical properties of objects and materials)* | Continue to share other board books with simple pictures. Encourage him to listen as I name objects or ask, "Where's the…?" |

Reading with **toddlers** is much more interactive. When you ask, "What's that?" they respond with a sound or a word or by pointing a finger. They also chime in with refrains, such as by chanting "E-I-E-I-O" as you read *Old McDonald.* They like books with pages they can turn, illustrations they can point to as you ask questions, and predictable phrases that are sometimes silly. As they grow older, they begin to select books on the basis of content, and they enjoy books with repetition, rhymes, and nonsense words.

Toddlers enjoy stories about families; feelings; animals; and everyday experiences such as taking a bath, going to bed, or missing mommy and daddy. Introduce books with simple concepts about size, shape, and color; alphabet books with simple, colorful illustrations; and books that answer questions about how things work.

Here are some tips for reading with toddlers:

**Encourage toddlers to look at the illustrations** as you read the text. For example, prompt, "Can you find Spot in the picture? Point to the dog."

**Ask simple questions** to help children understand what is being read, even if they cannot express themselves verbally yet. For example, prompt, "They're going bye-bye, aren't they? Can you wave bye-bye like the mommy in the story?"

**Read books with favorite stories, songs, or fingerplays** that they can join in telling or acting out, such as "Itsy-Bitsy Spider," or "Row, Row, Row Your Boat."

**Relate the story to the children's own lives.** For example, you might comment, "You have a dog, just like the boy in the story."

| Observe | Reflect | Respond |
|---|---|---|
| Tamika and Jorge join in as you read *Brown Bear, Bear Bear, What Do You See?* Tamika turns the pages and points to each new animal, waiting for you to say *red bird* or *yellow duck.* | Tamika turns the pages of the board book and notices and points to pictures. *(Objective 7, Demonstrates fine motor strength and coordination; Objective 8, Listens to and understands increasingly complex language)* | Share other books with simple rhymes (for example, *Polar Bear, Polar Bear, What Do You Hear?* and *Peek-a-Who?*) |

**Two-year-olds** enjoy listening to stories. They especially like stories about children and animals whose daily lives are similar to their own. They identify easily with mice who have grandmothers and children who are learning to use the potty.

By the time they are 2 years old, children who have frequently heard books read aloud bring favorite books to you again and again. They are ready to complete rhymes or fill in words you omit as you read familiar stories to them. They may begin pretending to read to you, to a friend, or to a doll by telling parts of a familiar story. Many twos will listen to entire stories, following simple plots. They participate in book-related experiences such as seeing what they can spy after listening to *Each Peach Pear Plum* by Janet and Allen Ahlberg or acting out a story such as Eric Carle's *From Head to Toe.*

| Observe | Reflect | Respond |
|---|---|---|
| Jorge fills in the missing rhyme when I omit it from the phrase "looking at *me.*" He points to each picture and names each animal and its color in Spanish. Then he names the animal in English. | Jorge is supplying the last word in the rhyme, now that we have read the book together many times. *(Objective 18, Comprehends and responds to books and other texts)*<br><br>He is speaking both Spanish and English. *(Objective 9, Uses spoken language to express thoughts and needs; Objective 38, Demonstrates progress in speaking English)* | Ask Jorge's father, Jose, to tape his reading of *Oso pardo, oso pardo, ¿qué ves ahí? (Brown Bear* written in Spanish). |

**Preschool children** enjoy exploring many kinds of stories and books. Some books remind them of the things they do every day or of special events in their lives. Some tell stories about things that are not real. Children this age have definite favorites and enjoy looking at and hearing them read again and again.

Their longer attention spans enable them to listen to longer stories, and their increased language skills enable them to talk with you about stories. Include a variety of books in your collection for preschool children, including narrative, predictable, alphabet, number/counting, informational, and rhyming books. While they still enjoy stories about families, homes, and friends, preschool children also appreciate stories with humor and a surprise ending, and imaginative stories that they know could never happen. Many preschool children like fairy tales, folktales, fables, and other fantasy stories, although some may be afraid of the monsters or wicked characters in these stories. Narratives help children learn that a story has a beginning, middle, and end.

Nonfiction books about topics that relate to children's current interests and books that introduce new topics and ideas help expand children's understanding of the world. Reference books such as simple picture dictionaries, software manuals, nature guides, and cookbooks help children learn that they can use books to find the information they want.

Preschool children pay attention to words, and they love stories with word plays, puns, and silly riddles. Nonsense rhymes, songbooks, and poetry are often popular with this age-group. Books with predictable language, lots of repetition, rhymes, and refrains engage children in interactive reading. They also enjoy books with cumulative text, where part of the text is repeated and one sentence is added on each page (such as *My Little Sister Ate One Hare* by Bill Grossman). Less-predictable books with somewhat more complex language and vocabulary gently challenge children and support their development of comprehension skills.

Here are some strategies for reading with preschool children:

**Read books that introduce new concepts** through pictures and simple language.

**Help children increase their vocabularies** by reading books that have more extensive vocabularies than their current listening and speaking vocabularies.

**Begin by talking about the book's cover.** For example, you might prompt, "This book is called *Caps for Sale*. Why do you think the man is in the tree?"

**Help children focus their attention and begin to predict the story:** "Poor Corduroy lost his button. I wonder where it is."

**Encourage children to use the illustrations** to understand what is going on in the story, to make predictions, and to check their comprehension: "Where are the children now? What do you think will happen to the little girl now that it is raining?"

**After reading the story once, ask questions while you read it again**: "Do you remember what the caterpillar eats next?' Ask children to talk about the characters, the plot, feelings, and concepts.

**Appeal to the children's sense of humor.** Skip an expected phrase or part of a familiar story from time to time so the children can enjoy catching your "mistakes." Switch words or play with words in fun ways.

**Pause** to enable children to anticipate dialog or join in saying refrains.

**Point out words** in the text as you read, and sometimes **run your finger along the text** to show the direction you are following. Encourage children to point to the words, too.

**Follow up** the story by reminding the child of the book during related activities or when the child is experiencing feelings similar to those of a book character. For example, when a child is upset, explain, "You're angry, just like Sophie."

| Observe | Reflect | Respond |
|---|---|---|
| Keisha is "reading" *The Three Little Pigs* to Rosa and Nathan. She holds the book up with the pages facing the other children. As she tells the story, she shows them the pictures and runs her finger under the words. She begins the story by saying, "Once upon a time..." | Keisha knows that many stories start with the phrase "Once upon a time" and that print is read from top to bottom and left to right. *(Objective 17, Demonstrates knowledge of print and its use; Objective 18, Comprehends and responds to books and other texts)* | Put out other books with stories she knows and that she can retell (for example, *The Gingerbread Boy, Hansel and Gretel,* and *Three Billy Goats Gruff.)* Put out a flannel board with pieces she can use to retell the stories. Encourage her to continue telling stories to Rosa and Nathan. |

**School-age children** have a wide range of interests and reading abilities. Most 5-year-olds are on the verge of reading. First graders are taking the enormous step of putting all of their emerging literacy skills together and figuring out their first books. An older school-age child may stumble through books while another reads with ease and comprehension. How do you select books for such a varied group? Fortunately, school-age children will be able to let you know what they are reading in school, what they like to read about, and who their favorite authors are.

Here are some guidelines to help you choose and suggest books for school-age children:

- Young school-age children enjoy many of the same books preschool children like. This is especially true of books with humor and irony.

- Books known as *early readers* are especially appropriate for children who are beginning to read. These books tend to be illustrated well and written simply.

- Many children's classics interest 8- to 10-year-old children. Adventure stories, mysteries, fairy tales, folktales, and exciting chapter books appeal to this age-group. Less-skilled readers delight and benefit from listening to these stories read aloud. Stronger readers will want to read and reread these books, themselves.

- Keep up with new books and the latest authors. Many newspapers review new children's books in their weekly book review sections. Consult booklists developed by experts, such as lists published by the International Reading Association (IRA). Look for Newberry Medal winners, which are identified by the American Library Association as being the most distinguished contributions to American literature for children.

- Suggest books that are related to what children are studying in school or to studies that you are doing in your family child care program. *The Creative Curriculum Study Starters* include lists of children's books related to particular study topics.

School-age children learn much of the content of academic subjects by reading textbooks. While you do not want to make your family child care home into a second school for your school-age children, it is very important for you to support their interest in books, their enjoyment of reading, and their language and literacy skills—especially their ability to understand what they read. You want to make homework and leisure reading as manageable and exciting as possible.

Here are some strategies you can use to bring language and literacy to life for school-age children:

**Be a good role model as a reader.** Show how reading is part of your life. Talk about what you read in newspapers, books, and magazines. Look at cookbooks with the children and find recipes to try. Answer children's questions by looking up information in an atlas, almanac, or online resource. Share books you loved as a child.

**Make library visits a regular part of your program.** Make sure that your school-age children get a library card as soon as they can write their names. That is when most libraries allow children to have cards.

**Encourage creative experiences related to books.** Children can put on a play for younger children, complete with a script, scenery, costumes, and a video of the play to show later. They can write new endings to favorite books or write whole new versions by setting the stories in different eras. They might investigate the historical context of a book, find out about the author, or make a commercial to convince other children to read a favorite book.

**Help school-age children start book collections of their own,** perhaps beginning with books about a hobby or books by a favorite author. Start a book club with school-age children in other family child care programs. They can write about books and send reviews to each other through the Internet. The "In2Books" program links children in grades 3–5 with trained, adult pen pals who read and correspond online about particular books. That program has a home version that can be used in family child care programs.

**Encourage school-age children to share their skills.** Teach them some of the ways you make reading interactive and invite them to read to the younger children. Provide supplies for them to write and illustrate original picture books or make "feely" books for infants by sewing fabrics or unbreakable objects, such as a rattle or pacifier, onto cloth pages. Let them become the writers for preschool children's dictation.

**Encourage creative writing.** Introduce poetry forms such as haiku and limericks. Have children interview family members about their lives and write a biography of a parent, grandparent, aunt, uncle, or cousin. Challenge them to invent new superheroes or tall tale characters and write stories about them. Let them publish your FCC newsletter.

**Play word games.** Encourage children to make up riddles and language codes, and to write sentences using words that all begin with the same letter (for example, "Big, bold brown bear broke baby's bowling ball," or "Calico cats can construct cool coconut cookies."). Play "Scrabble®" and "Boggle®" and offer crossword puzzles. Introduce them to the children's version of Lynne Truss's book *Eats, Shoots & Leaves* and have them make up their own sentences that show why commas make a difference.

| Observe | Reflect | Respond |
|---|---|---|
| Tyrone arrives in the afternoon, excited about a book that he read last night. He tells you that it's called *Shiloh* and that it's the story of a brave boy who rescues a dog from a man who mistreated it. | Tyrone is a good reader and gets excited about what he reads. He loves animals and reads both fiction and nonfiction about them. | Encourage Tyrone to read some of his favorite picture books about animals to the other children. Invite him to write a story about his dog, Bailey. Suggest that he read other books by Phyllis Reynolds Naylor and decide if she is one of his favorite authors. |

## Including All Children

You can make sure that all children have enjoyable experiences with stories and books, including children whose home languages are not English and including children with disabilities. The general strategies that you use for sharing stories and books promote the skills and interests of all children. Here are some additional suggestions for making experiences with stories and books meaningful for all children.

**If a child speaks a language other than English,** try these strategies:

- Read the story to the child in his or her home language before reading it in English, or have family members read it to the child first in their home language.

- Introduce key words and phrases in English and convey the meaning with gestures and pictures.

- Use pictures and props to help children understand the text.

- Allow children to respond in their home languages or nonverbally.

- Select books with rhymes and repetition, which enable children to follow along more easily. Dual-language learners often recite familiar phrases of books before they begin expressing their own ideas in English.

- Keep story time short and select books with easy-to-follow story lines. This is particularly important for children who are in the early stages of learning English.

- Include books with photographs that show the cultures of the children in your program respectfully. It is important for dual-language learners to see people who look like them and their families portrayed positively in books.

**If a child shows variable attention during story time,** try these strategies:

- Encourage the child's engagement with stories by offering hands-on experiences. For example, cut pictures from a book, laminate them for long-term use, and attach them with VELCRO® to the same picture in another copy of the book. The child can interact by pulling them off or putting them on when you read the story.

- Provide touch-and-feel or scratch-and-sniff books for children to explore.

- Offer story-related props so that children have something to hold and manipulate.

- Share books that encourage children to move.

**If a child has difficulty hearing, understanding, or seeing books,** try these strategies:

- Have the child sit close to you.
- Repeat words and phrases to offer extra time for comprehension.
- Use exaggerated facial expressions, vocal tones, and gestures when reading.
- Use peer buddies to support children while they look at books.
- Offer books of various sizes and with textures and sounds that engage children.
- Use books with large print, raised textures, and tactile illustrations to prepare children's fingers for Braille.

**If a child has trouble holding and manipulating reading materials,** try these strategies:

- Use book trays or book holders.
- Attach VELCRO® tabs on pages to make turning them easier.
- Use peer buddies who will help turn pages.
- Provide recordings, a tape or CD player, and headphones as another way for children to hear stories read aloud.
- Use computer storybooks with accessible technology.

## Engaging Children of All Ages

Books can be used in a variety of ways, at different times of the day, and with all age-groups. Here is an example of what might take place in your family child care home.

Rosa (4 years) and Tamika (19 months) arrive at your home at 6:45 a.m. After friendly greetings, they settle on the couch to look at books. Keisha (4 ½ years) joins them after pulling one from the shelf near the couch where you keep books for the children.

"Read, read," Tamika says as she waves her favorite book. She hands the book to Keisha, who loves pretending to be a teacher and "reading" to the other children.

"Not again!" Keisha pretends to protest as she smiles. "*Spot's Baby Sister* again? We read that yesterday and the day before and the day before! Okay, here we go. I'll read, and you can open the flaps and turn the pages. Be careful. Don't tear the book. Rosa, you may listen, too."

Although she cannot read the words yet, Keisha has memorized the book. She tells the story, involves Tamika while she's reading, and encourages Rosa to point to and name things in the pictures. The children enjoy this transitional routine every morning. You enjoy the routine because it gives you a few minutes to talk with Tamika's and Rosa's parents before they gently interrupt the story to say good-bye. After one or two books, the children are ready to have breakfast and join the other children who have arrived.

Later that day, Tyrone (8 years) says, "Growl, growl, somebody's been sitting in my chair!" He pretends to be the papa bear from *Goldilocks and the Three Bears*, which you have read to the younger children many times.

"Somebody's been sitting in my chair," exclaims Keisha, pretending to be the mama bear.

"Somebody's been sitting in my chair, and now it's broken," you say in your highest baby-bear voice. The children giggle about the way you are speaking. Tamika, Jorge (2 ½ years), Nathan (3 years), and Rosa join you in saying, "Waa, waa, waa," pretending to cry like baby bear.

"And the three bears went upstairs," prompts Tyrone, an accomplished reader who is narrating the children's enactment of the story. They use props and continue to adopt bear voices. Jeremy (8 months) is lying on his tummy on the floor nearby, examining vinyl books. When the older children talk about Baby Bear, they look at Jeremy and remind Mama Bear or Papa Bear to bring him on the walk.

When the day is almost over, you tell the children, "Your families will be here pretty soon. It's time to choose the book you want to take home tonight." As the children make their choices, you have them sign library forms and put their books in their backpacks. "I hope their families don't mind reading *Spot's Baby Sister* or *The Three Bears* again," you think to yourself with a smile. Tyrone takes *Donovan and the Word Jar*, the chapter book that he has been reading with his parents. "My parents love this book," he reports. "I wonder what word we'll put in *our* word jar tonight. Last night we put the word *entomology* in the jar after we watched the fireflies.

This is an example of how stories and books can be woven into experiences with children of different ages throughout the day. It illustrates several points:

- Books are extremely useful during transitional times and to help children understand and manage their feelings.

- Books can be used independently and in groups, providing children with rich learning experiences.

- Because little preparation is required and no cleanup is needed other than putting the books away, reading can be done at any time and in any place, in addition to the formal read-aloud times you schedule.

- Books can help strengthen the ties between your family child care program and the children's families.

# Partnering With Families

Families will be pleased that you have a good supply of books in your home and that you read to children often. You can share what you are doing by using and sending home *LearningGames®* activities and by sending the letter to families about stories and books.

## *LearningGames®* for Stories and Books

### Birth–12 months

**Game 19, "Reading Pictures and Books"**

It's never too soon to start looking at books with babies. Families can enjoy books with their infants as you do in your program. Help families get babies off to a good start with books by sharing this *LearningGames* activity with them. Explain that looking at cards and board books with simple pictures is an important step in children's literacy development.

### 12– 24 months

**Game 67, "See, Show, Say"**

Help families learn the "3S" technique for interactive story reading: see, show, say. Those actions are three levels of response to a prompt, and each type of response is more challenging than the last. Model the technique for families before sending this activity home. First, ask the child to notice a picture (see): "Do you see the doggy?" Next, invite the child to point to a picture (show): "Where's the doggie?" Then encourage the child to name the object or to answer a simple question (say): "What kind of animal is that?"

24–36 months

### Game 75, "Sharing Nursery Rhymes"

Families enjoy sharing their favorite nursery rhymes with their children. Children love the sounds and rhythm of nursery rhymes, so they chant and clap along. Nursery rhymes are a great way for families to share their languages, traditions, and cultures. Share the nursery rhyme books that you have in your reading area so families can also learn the rhymes you say in your program.

36–48 months

### Game 115, "Stories With Three"

Isn't it amazing how many children's stories involve groups of three? *The Three Little Pigs, The Three Billy Goats Gruff*, and *The Three Bears* are just a few. Encourage families to read stories with groups of three to their 3-year-olds and to count items in the story, such as the bears' bowls, chairs, and beds, just as you do in your program. Three is a significant number for 3-year-olds, and they can count groups of three throughout the day. For example, their families can encourage them to take three crackers for a snack and choose three books to look at before bed.

48–60 months

### Game 171, "Add to the Tale"

This game shows another way for you to make story reading interactive. Children and families can have fun together, telling what might happen to story characters after the original story ends. Does Goldilocks come back to the three bears' house? Do the bears visit Goldilocks' house? Encourage families to help children predict will happen next while listening to a story and to imagine what might happen if they extend the story beyond the author's ending.

[1] National Association for Family Child Care. (2005). *Quality standards for NAFCC accreditation* (4th ed.). [Electronic version]. Retrieved February 8, 2009, from http://www.nafcc.org/accreditation/accredstandards.asp.

# A Letter to Families About Stories and Books

Dear Families,

Reading is essential for school success. It's also a wonderful source of enjoyment. Reading to children every day is one of the best ways to interest children in books, and it can be among the most treasured times you have together.

I have a large collection of books for the children, and we go to the library regularly for story time and to find more books. I encourage the children to look at books whenever they want, and we read together at least once a day. Sometimes I choose a story to read to the children. At other times, I let them pick their favorites.

Reading aloud encourages children to love books, introduces new ideas, and helps children learn how to handle problems. As children listen to me read and look at the pictures and text, their own reading skills begin to develop.

- We look at the pictures together, and I ask them questions like these: "Can you find where the caterpillar is now?" or "What is that silly dog doing?"
- I point out the pictures to infants and tell them what objects are called.
- I ask the older children, "What do you think will happen next?" or "Why do you think she's smiling?" Questions like that help them understand the story and learn about story structure.
- I let all the children help me tell the story by repeating words or phrases they remember from previous readings. Sometimes rhymes and refrains also help them predict the text as we read together.
- I encourage children to look at books, listen to recorded stories, retell stories, and scribble and write throughout the day. Sometimes children dictate stories to me.

Read and tell stories to your child every day. Reading aloud together and telling stories lets your child know how much you value these activities, and their enjoyment of books encourages them to learn to read. Here are some more things you can do with your child.

- Encourage your child to talk about the stories you read.
- Offer prompts such as "I wonder what will happen next?" or "I wonder why..."
- Try to relate the story to something in your child's life: "That dog looks just like Grandpa's."
- Let your child experiment with paper and pencils, pens, or markers.
- Take your child to the library for story time and to check out books.

Let's share information. I can tell you the titles of the books your child enjoys here, and you can tell me your child's favorite story or nursery rhyme so I can read or recite it, too. If you record your child's favorite story or nursery rhyme, I can play it during the day, especially if you speak a language at home that I don't speak.

Sincerely,

# Sand and Water

**15**

# Sand and Water

Tamika (19 months) toddles over to you, holding her favorite doll. She lifts the doll toward you, shakes it, and smiles. As you take the doll from her, she points to the doll's dirty legs and says, "Uh-oh."

Noting the dirt, you say, "Your baby doll is very dirty. She needs a bath! Let's get some soap and water so you can wash her." Taking Tamika to the kitchen, you place a plastic tub filled with an inch of warm water on a vinyl tablecloth on the floor. Then you hand her a wet washcloth and her doll. Tamika puts the doll in the water and starts bouncing it. At your suggestion, she wipes the doll's legs with the washcloth. Tamika continues bouncing the doll in the water, clearly enjoying herself.

Young children are usually very attracted to water and sand. There is something about splashing water and sifting sand that almost everyone finds appealing. Even as an adult, there may be times when you crave a warm bath or a walk on a sandy beach. Sand and water are soothing and relaxing for people of all ages.

Besides being calming activities, playing with sand and water leads to interesting discoveries. As they pour and splash, sift and build, children learn the difference between wet and dry. They can hide things in sand but not in clear water. They also observe how food coloring or detergent makes water colorful or bubbly and that adding water to sand makes it stick together so they can mold it. Children fill and empty pails, pitchers, and cups endlessly. Playing with sand and water teaches science and math concepts in meaningful ways.

# Setting Up for Sand and Water Play

Of course, if you're going to let children play with sand and water, you want them to be able to play freely without worrying about accidental splashes and spills. Some providers are reluctant to include sand and water play in their programs because those activities are messy. However, it is not difficult to minimize messes, and planning makes cleanup easier.

## Choosing Materials and Equipment

Here are some considerations for indoor sand and water play:

**Make use of your kitchen and bathroom for sand and water play.** These rooms are designed for cleaning spills easily. Kitchen and bathroom sinks are ideal places for individual water play. Plastic dish tubs or trays can also be set on the floor for individual play experiences with water or sand.

**You do not have to purchase commercial tables for group play.** Think about using a very small wading pool on your kitchen floor for water play. Alternatively, you can construct outdoor sand and water containers by building wooden boxes lined with plastic. Five feet by five feet is a good size to consider. For sand play, fill the box with dry, finely textured white sand. Bags of sterilized white play sand can be purchased at lumber or building supply stores. The ground is fine for digging, but backyard dirt does not work well in tables and tubs.

**Protect play areas to make cleanup easier.** Even though the kitchen and bathroom are relatively easy to clean up, you will find the job much easier if you prepare the rooms for water or sand spills. Toweling, a sheet of plastic, an old shower curtain, oilcloth tablecloths, or vinyl crib pads will protect the floor. If children spill water, you can mop it up readily. For sand play, place towels or bath mats under the sand tubs or trays. They will keep the sand localized. When the children are finished, you can fold the towel or mat and shake it outside. To prevent tripping, keep the edges of the protective covering taped down while the children are playing.

To offer sand and water play outdoors, consider what is already available in your backyard as well as easy additions. Here are some suggestions:

**Offer opportunities for digging.** Children can dig directly in the ground or in a sandbox. If you do not have a sandbox, a tractor tire makes a sturdy sandbox frame. Fill sandboxes or frames with sterilized white sand, as described above.

**Use hoses and sprinklers on hot days.** Carefully supervised wading pools are excellent water tubs.

**Build group sand or water tubs with wood and line them with plastic,** as mentioned above.

Whether you offer sand and water play indoors or outdoors (or, even better, in both), you'll need to protect children's clothing. Children's aprons can be made from old shower curtains, heavy-duty garbage bags, or old raincoats. Adding VELCRO™ closures makes it easy for children to put smocks on and take them off by themselves. Some providers have children wear rubber boots or put plastic bags over their shoes for water play. Of course, bare feet and swimming suits are another option. You should always have a spare set of clothes for every child.

Because babies put sand—and everything else—in their mouths, it is best not to introduce sand play until children are about a year old. You will find, though, that even the very youngest infants can begin to enjoy water play. Once babies can sit up, you can give them a small basin with about an inch of water and some plastic cups or a rubber duck.

Props enhance sand and water play. For older infants, toddlers, and twos, offer plastic bottles, washable dolls, funnels, and floating toys for water play. You can add to this inventory with props picked up at yard sales or dollar stores. These materials will interest young children during water play:

| | | |
|---|---|---|
| basters | measuring cups | sieves |
| bottle brushes | measuring spoons and slotted spoons | small pots and pans |
| buckets, pails, and mixing bowls | paint brushes | toy vehicles |
| colanders | ping pong balls | whisks |
| corks | plastic bottles, pitchers, and jugs | |
| foam alphabet letters | | |
| ladles | | |
| rubber or plastic animal and people figurines | | |

For sand play, young children enjoy many of the same props used in water play, such as rubber or plastic figurines, measuring cups and spoons, buckets and pails, and colanders. In addition, these props will enrich their play:

| | | |
|---|---|---|
| collectibles, such as large shells, that do not pose choking hazards | scoops and small shovels | sifters |
| | shakers with large holes | small wheelbarrows |
| craft sticks | shovels, spoons, and scoops of various sizes | |
| molds and muffin tins | | |

Older children also love to experiment, explore, and investigate. They use sand and water for imaginary play. Props make their play more exciting and complex. In addition to the props used by younger children, these enhance preschool children's water play:

| | | |
|---|---|---|
| bubble solutions and various wands, including fruit containers and straws | plastic dishes | sponges |
| | plastic straws | strainers |
| | siphons and tubing | toothbrushes |
| eye droppers | small water pumps | water mills (water wheels) |
| fishing bobbers | spray bottles | watering cans |
| fishnets | | |
| fizzy bath balls | | |
| funnels | | |

Sand props that older children enjoy and learn with include

| | | |
|---|---|---|
| cookie cutters | magnetic wands | rakes and shovels |
| feathers | magnifying glasses | sand mills (sand wheels) |
| flags | marbles | sifters |

School-age children enjoy special activities and projects, such as blowing oversized bubbles, sculpting and casting sand, and sand painting. The materials you need for their play will, of course, correspond to the projects they enjoy. For example, if children want to make bubbles of varying shapes and sizes, you might assemble these supplies:

| | | |
|---|---|---|
| wire and wire cutters | plastic berry containers | glycerin |
| empty eyeglass frames | coat hangers | recipe for making a solution for monster bubbles |
| plastic rings from six-packs | liquid soap | |

## Monster Bubble Solution

Combine 6 cups of distilled water, ¾ cup of light corn syrup, and 2 cups of dishwashing liquid in a container. Mix well. Let the solution sit for 4 hours before using it.

## Displaying Props

When you set up for sand and water play, think about both your indoor and outdoor environments. Props should be within children's reach so they can choose what they want to use. Here are ways to display materials:

- Place props at the children's eye level so they can see what is available.
  - Make use of a hook system for hanging mesh bags filled with props.
  - Use narrow drawers or boxes to hold collectibles such as shells, marbles, or coins. Remember to keep items that children can choke on out of their reach.

- Store props in shoe boxes or plastic containers by function. For example, one box might have props for filling, such as scoops, measuring cups, and shovels. Another box might have items of various weights for sinking and floating experiments, such as corks, feathers, marbles, and small pieces of wood. Take a photo or draw a picture of what is kept inside each box and tape the picture and a written descriptor on the outside of the box. You may want to cover the labels with clear contact paper or tape to protect them from moisture.

## Alternatives to Sand Play

In the past you may have used or noticed that others provide rice, macaroni, dried beans, or dried corn kernels in the sand table. These are interesting substitutes for sand, especially when you dye them bright colors. You need to be wary of these materials, though. If you have infants and toddlers in your program, remember that uncooked rice, pasta, beans, and corn are potential choking hazards. Even if your program only serves older children, using food as a substitute for sand is not always a good idea. As noted in chapter 12, "Art," many people have strong reservations about using food for anything other than eating. Before using rice, pasta, beans, or corn for a sensory experience, check with the children's families to make sure they support this use of food.

Better yet, think of some non-food materials. Torn newspaper, packing "peanuts," and recycled tire mulch are interesting alternatives to sand. You might also want to use aluminum pie weights or colored stones sold for fish tanks and flower arranging. When you look for interesting materials don't forget natural alternatives like snow.

# Caring and Teaching

If you have prepared well to minimize messes, children will have the freedom thoroughly to enjoy playing with sand and water, and you can share their delight. As always, your first consideration should be children's health and safety.

## Keeping Children Safe and Healthy

- Supervise children closely. Children have been known to drown in less than an inch of water.

- If you are using the kitchen or bathroom for sand and water play, make sure that the areas are childproofed. This means that all hazardous items, such as razors, knives, and cleaning agents, have been locked away. Empty outlets must be covered, and electrical appliances such as hair dryers should be put away to guard against having wet hands come in contact with electricity.

- If you use a sink for water play, you may need to provide step stools with rubber slats so that children can play comfortably at the sink.

- To prevent scalding accidents, the American Burn Association recommends that hot water be set at no more than 110 degrees F in a child care facility. This is especially important if you care for babies because an infant's skin is 15 times thinner than an adult's. In fact, the Association recommends 100 degrees F as the safe bathing temperature for adults.[1]

- Use fresh water in tubs and trays. Empty all water after each use.

- Children engaged in group water play need to be free of cuts, scratches, and sores on their hands, and they must not have colds and runny noses.

- Children need to wash their hands before and after participating in group water play.

- Sanitize water tubs and props after each use, using a mild bleach solution of 1 tablespoon of liquid chlorine bleach to 1 gallon of water (or 1 teaspoon of liquid chlorine bleach to 1 quart of water). Do not add the bleach solution to the water in the table or tub.

- Cover outdoor sandboxes when not in use to keep animals out of them.

## Responding to Each Child

Sand and water play are so enjoyable, adults sometimes forget how much children learn during these experiences. Always bear in mind that sand and water are wonderful for science experiments, learning about math and the arts, and developing language and social skills.

When young **infants** are first introduced to water, they approach it with all of their senses. As they pour, poke, splash, and even taste water, they acquire information about it. You can help children at this early stage of development interact with water by describing what you see them doing.

| Observe | Reflect | Respond |
|---|---|---|
| On a hot summer day, you sit in the backyard wading pool, holding Jeremy in your lap. Jeremy takes great delight in splashing the water with his arms. | Jeremy is using his large muscles as he waves his arms to splash the water. (*Objective 6, Demonstrates gross motor manipulative skills*) | Comment on Jeremy's actions: "Look at the big splashes you make when your hand hits the water!" Encourage Jeremy to try splashing with his legs and then with both his arms and legs: "Jeremy, let's see what will happen when you kick your legs in the water." |

**Toddlers and twos** know what sand and water are like, and they enjoy experimenting. They discover that adding food coloring changes the color of water and that adding a little water to sand makes the sand too hard to pour. To promote learning during sand and water play, talk with toddlers and twos about what they are doing. Ask them questions that will encourage them to observe and explore.

| Observe | Reflect | Respond |
| --- | --- | --- |
| For a new experience, you added water to the sand in a tub. Jorge has been using a cookie cutter to make sand "cookies." He brings one to his lips; says, "Mmmm"; and pretends to chew his "cookie." | Jorge made sand cookies and is enjoying a pretend treat. *(Objective 14, Uses symbols and images to represent something not present)* | Join Jorge to extend his play. Say, "Those cookies look yummy, Jorge. May I join you? Let's pour some milk to drink with our cookies." |

**Preschool children** are intentional in their play. For example, they might get a comb to etch designs in the sand. They also engage in imaginary play. A pile of sand can become a castle, including a moat and a tunnel. The water table may turn into a sea where rubber people dive for sparkling treasures like shiny dimes. To enhance preschoolers' play with sand and water, pose questions that will help them relate new and previous experiences, solve problems, and use their developing skills.

| Observe | Reflect | Respond |
|---|---|---|
| Rosa has been cleaning a small pile of river stones with a toothbrush. She drops the clean stones one by one into a tank of water, which she calls her rock garden. Each time a stone hits the bottom, she claps, looks at you, and says, "¡Se hundió"! | Rosa is learning about the physical attributes of rocks and water by using a tool and by experimenting with them. *(Objective 26, Demonstrates knowledge of the physical properties of objects and materials; Objective 28, Uses tools and other technology to perform tasks)*<br><br>As she drops rocks into the water, she is making scientific observations. *(Objective 11, Demonstrates positive approaches to learning; Objective 24, Uses scientific inquiry skills)* | Comment on what Rosa is doing and lead her to a higher level of investigation: "Yes, Rosa, the rocks sank. When you're done sinking those rocks, let's see whether some other objects will sink or float. Here's a sponge. Do you think it will sink like the rocks or float on top of the water?" |

**School-age children** are not likely to want to play with sand and water in the same ways as the younger children. Their investigations go beyond seeing what will sink or float. They might be more interested in an experiment to grow plants hydroponically (that is, using water, light, and mineral nutrients without soil). To entertain the younger children and themselves, they may create bubble frames and blow enormous bubbles.

| Observe | Reflect | Respond |
|---|---|---|
| Tyrone has been helping the younger children blow bubbles outdoors. After a while he tells you he wants to do something different that will still be fun for them but more interesting for him. | You refer to this book for ideas that will excite him. Together you read about making humongous monster bubbles. Tyrone thinks that idea is perfect. | Help Tyrone assemble the necessary supplies and mix the bubble solution. (See page 307 for a bubble solution recipe.)<br><br>After school the next day, gather the children for a special surprise. Introduce Tyrone and his monster bubbles with great fanfare. |

## Engaging Children of All Ages

Because sand and water play are potentially messy and chaotic, it is important to plan for and supervise the children's play. Here is an example of how to do this.

---

Catching your eye, Jorge (2 ½ years) starts pushing the kitchen step stool over to the sink. He climbs halfway up before turning to you and saying, "Abra. We play water."

Quickly you assess whether this is a good time for water play. The two babies are napping, and Keisha (4 ½ years) is sitting at the dining room table. She is listening to an audiotape of the story you read aloud in the morning, but she is clearly watching what Jorge is doing. Rosa (4 years) is also at the table, putting a puzzle together. You decide that now is a good time. "Okay, Jorge, you may play with water," you tell him.

"Yes, play water!" Jorge agrees enthusiastically.

"First we have to get some towels. Follow me." Cooperating, Jorge follows you to the linen closet, from which you take two towels and a plastic apron. "Here you go. You may carry these," you say as you hand him the towels. Jorge happily marches back to the kitchen with the towels.

Then you spread one towel on the floor and put one on the counter for spills. After you help Jorge put the apron on, he quickly moves the chair near the sink and climbs back on it. As you close the drain, you say, "Let's put some water in the sink so you can play. What would you like to put in the water?"

"Spoon," answers Jorge, so you hand one to him.

"Would you like these plastic measuring cups, too?" you ask.

"Si", he responds, nodding his head enthusiastically.

"How does the water feel?" you ask, engaging him in conversation.

"Cold and mojado", he responds as he spills the water from the measuring cup over his hand."

"Yes, it is cold and wet. Let's count how many spoons of water it takes to fill the cup," you suggest. Together you count to six in Spanish and then in English, noting the height of the water in the cup as Jorge adds each spoonful.

As Jorge empties the cup and starts over, you decide that he has everything he needs for water play. You turn to Keisha, who has been watching the action from the dining room table: "Keisha, would you like to play at other sink, next to Jorge?"

"Yes," responds Keisha, "but I need to do something more grown-up because I'm more bigger."

"What might that be?" you inquire with a smile.

She answers, "Remember when we made the water go through a tube for a fountain? I want to do that."

"One fountain, coming up!" you announce as you head to the cabinet for tubing.

This scenario illustrates several important points:

- Water play requires supervision. You do not want to leave young children near water by themselves.

- Props enhance water play.

- Children learn science and math concepts through water play.

- Children do not need to be doing the same things. This is especially important to remember when you care for children of different ages and developmental levels.

- Your conversations with children not only promote language development, but they encourage children to be better observers and help children connect new experiences with previous experiences.

- It is important to encourage dual-language learners like Jorge to speak in both their home languages and English.

## Partnering With Families

Children can play with sand and water at home as easily as in your program. The following *LearningGames®* activities and the letter to families about sand and water will help families understand the value of sand and water play.

### *LearningGames®* for Sand and Water

Birth–12 months

**Game 24, "Dropping Objects"**

Young babies can hold things well, but they cannot always let them go. This game helps them strengthen and control the muscles in their hands. When children are washing their hands or playing with water, encourage them to drop objects and watch the splashes they make. Encourage families to play this game during bath time. Dropping objects in water makes fun splashes that may encourage babies to continue practicing their new skill.

12–24 months

### Game 45, "Water Play"

Every home has opportunities for water play. Encourage families to let children linger for a moment while they are washing their hands, play outside with a dishpan partly filled with water, pour water into plastic cups, or splash around in the bathtub. Young children enjoy water because it moves in unexpected ways. Show families how you place plastic dishpans on a towel for water play in your program.

24–36 months

### Game 69, "Create a Face"

Encourage families to try "Another idea" for this *LearningGame* activity by inviting their child to draw faces in sand. While sand is not recommended for infants because they put it in their mouths, 2-year-olds enjoy exploring sand. Creating a face is only one of many things children this age can do with sand. Encourage families to let their children play in an indoor or outdoor sandbox with a variety of props, just as they do in your family child care program.

36–48 months

### Game 111, "Compare Two Amounts"

Water and sand are ideal for this *LearningGames* activity, which helps children understand *more* and *less*. First play the game with two containers of obviously different sizes. The larger cup will have more sand or water than the smaller cup when they are both filled to the top. Talk about which cup has more and which has less. Later play the game with two identical cups, but put more sand or water in one cup than in the other. Play these games with the preschool children in your program and encourage families to play them, too.

48–60 months

### Game 190, "Wondering What Caused It"

Ask children questions that prompt children to notice what happens and to think about why. Encourage families to ask their child questions such as these: What will happen to water if you put it in the freezer or leave it outdoors on a very cold day? Why does the water in the fish tank disappear? Why does the sand feel muddy now? What might happen if we forget to water our plants?

---

[1] American Burn Association. (n.d.). *Scald injury prevention* [PowerPoint presentation]. Retrieved February 11, 2009, from http://www.ameriburn.org/Prevent/PowerPoint/ScaldInjury_files.frame.htm.

# A Letter to Families About
# Sand and Water Play

Dear Families,

Although you're probably used to seeing your child splash in the bathtub and dig in a playground sandbox, you may not realize that we regularly play with sand and water at my home. We play with water indoors, using the kitchen or bathroom sink and small plastic tubs. We use sand in tubs and on trays. Outdoors, the children dig in the ground or use tubs filled with sand, water, and sometimes both!

When children pour water into measuring cups, they are exploring math concepts. When they drop corks, stones, feathers, and marbles into a tub of water, they are scientists, discovering which objects sink and which float. When they comb patterns in sand, they are exploring both math and art.

Children aren't always aware of what they are learning, so I help them talk about their observations. For example, I might say,

"Look how cloudy the water is with soap in it. You can't see the toys."

"You made the wheel turn by pouring sand through the top."

Sometimes I ask questions to extend the children's thinking, for example,

"How is wet sand different from dry sand?"

"How many cups of water do you think we have to pour into this jug to fill it?"

You can set up water and sand play for your child at home, much as I do. Here are some suggestions:

**Offer water play to children of all ages.** However, babies under 12 months shouldn't play with sand because they might swallow it.

**Prepare your home to make cleanup easy.** For water play, place a large towel on the floor and let your child use the bathroom or kitchen sink. For sand play, use a rubber dish pan placed on a towel on the floor. Your child does not need more than 2–3 inches of sand or water.

**Offer props to enrich play.** Give your child a baster, plastic measuring cups and spoons, a funnel, a sieve, plastic or rubber figurines and boats, a comb, pails and shovels, and squeeze bottles. These items will lead to many hours of enjoyment.

**Encourage your child to explore and experiment.** For a new experience, add soap flakes or food coloring to water. Try blowing bubbles by using different kinds of frames. Plastic six-pack rings, empty berry containers, or an eyeglass frame without the lenses can be used as bubble wands.

Sand and water play are a lot more than just fun. They are calming activities and important ways for children to develop thinking skills and explore math and science concepts.

Sincerely,

# Discovery

# Discovery

Keisha (4 ½ years) and Rosa (4 years) are taking apart a broken clock at the discovery table. Keisha says, "If you move this thing, that other thing will move. You try it."

Rosa moves the part again and again, watching what happens. Tyrone (8 years) joins them. "That's a gear," he explains. "When you move the small gear, the larger one moves, too. I have gears on my bike."

*Merriam-Webster's Collegiate Dictionary* defines *discover* as "to make known; to obtain knowledge of for the first time; to find out."[1] Children of all ages are curious and wonder about the world around them. They may think to themselves,

"I wonder what will happen if I push this button."

"I wonder what the bunny feels like."

"I wonder why my plant died."

"I wonder how I can make a bigger bubble."

When given opportunities to explore and discover, children build their social–emotional, physical, cognitive, and language skills. They learn to work together as they solve problems. They take care of living things such as pets and plants, and they learn how to use materials safely and responsibly. They develop fine motor skills when they use eyedroppers to squeeze colored water onto waxed paper or pick up a dead insect with tweezers. They build gross motor skills as they move their bodies to cast shadows on a wall or run in place before taking their pulses. Think of the many new words and concepts children learn as they explore scientific topics. For example, they learn that the caterpillar crawling along the ground goes through four stages as it transforms itself into a butterfly: egg, larva, pupa, and adult. They find out that flowers have many parts and learn that people who study flowers (and other plants) are called *botanists* while people who study rocks are called *geologists*.

# Setting Up for Discovery

You can set up a special place in your family child care home for discovery, a place for young children to explore science. Children discover by using their senses to touch, feel, taste, smell, and see. They act on objects and observe what happens. With your guidance, they can explore materials freely and learn to use tools.

A table set near a window and stocked with interesting materials and tools—a microscope, a magnifying glass, and a magnet— invites children to investigate. The window provides light for plants and for exploring shadows and reflections.

Of course, discovery experiences take place outdoors in your play yard or on a neighborhood walk as well as in your indoor discovery area. Chapter 20, "Outdoors," discusses experiences such as playing with natural materials, gardening, observing living things, caring for pets, and collecting. Think about what children are discovering outdoors as they dig and pour and as they roll, throw, bounce, and catch balls.

## Choosing Materials

**Infants and toddlers** need only simple materials that they can explore with all of their senses. As they mouth, shake, drop, and bang objects, they learn about physical properties such as weight, texture, and shape. They also learn what they can do with the objects. Balls roll. Rectangular blocks don't! A toy shopping cart is harder to push when it is filled with blocks than when it is empty.

Toss a ball into a big box or roll it through a tube and invite the children to look for it. A young child may expect to find the ball in the tube. Imagine his delight when it pops out the other end! Something different happens when you change the size of the ball or the tube, or when you vary the angle or height of the tube. Oops! A large ball got stuck, presenting an opportunity to solve a problem.

Consider **preschool and school-age children's** interests and experiences as you select materials. Nontoxic plants; an aquarium for fish or hermit crabs; or small pets such as guinea pigs, gerbils, hamsters, or even a rabbit help children learn to care for living things. Your collections of shells, rocks, bottle caps, and buttons will fascinate children, as will those nonworking but safe take-apart items you thought about tossing out: old clocks, telephones, radios, or toasters. Encourage children to bring treasures to share, such as abandoned nests or sea glass.

Here are some characteristics of good materials for children to explore:

**They are safe to use.** Keep these safety considerations in mind, especially if you include take-apart materials. Do not let children take apart computers or televisions. Always cut cords and remove batteries. Remove any glass, tubes, or bulbs. If you have a mixed age-group, keep materials with small parts that present choking hazards out of the reach of younger children. Provide safety goggles.

**They can be used in many different ways.** Materials that are open-ended promote discovery and exploration because there is no right or wrong way to use them. Children can make predictions, check whether their predictions were accurate, and see if they can figure out why things happen. Encourage children to investigate the materials: "The magnet attracts *(a nice new word)* paper clips, but it doesn't attract paper. I wonder what else it will attract."

**They challenge children to experiment and solve problems.** They challenge children to find answers to their own questions: "What would happen if…?" and "I wonder why…?"

**They change state.** Ice becomes a liquid as it melts. Liquid water becomes a solid when it freezes and a gas when it evaporates. Sugar and salt seem to disappear as they dissolve *(another nice new word!)*. Do they dissolve more quickly in cold or warm water?

**They help children make connections and think about big questions.** What do plants and animals need to grow? Do fish get hungry like we do? What happens to garbage after I throw it away? How did people live before there was electricity? Why are there so many kinds of rocks?

Provide basic tools for scientific exploration, such as magnifying glasses, balance scales, magnets, unbreakable thermometers, flashlights, mirrors, binoculars, eyedroppers, tweezers, screwdrivers, stethoscopes, and a digital camera. Remember that real tools work better than toy tools.

Include related nonfiction books as well as paper and writing tools so children can record their discoveries in words, charts, graphs, and pictures. A digital camera can help children keep track of how their seeds grow into plants or how the level of water in a bottle drops as it evaporates.

## Displaying Materials

A place for discovery can simply be a table to hold displays, collections, and tools; a shelf to store materials to explore; and trays to hold related materials. Include containers for sorting and classifying, and transform a plastic dishpan into a sensory tub. Children will have interesting experiences as they explore coffee grounds mixed with potting soil one week, a cornstarch and water mixture the next, and biodegradable packing materials a third. As usual, label shelves and containers with words and pictures.

# Caring and Teaching

Your own curiosity and your ability to ask children questions that promote their curiosity are all you need to encourage children to be investigators. You don't have to know answers to all of their questions. A "let's find out together" attitude shows children that we are always learning new things and that we can find information by observing, guessing, asking questions, experimenting, looking things up, and conducting investigations. Make the phrase "I wonder" part of your everyday speech.

The best questions are open-ended. These questions ask children to make predictions, consider consequences, think about things in new ways, apply what they already know to new situations, and solve problems. Here are some open-ended prompts:

- "What do you think will happen if..."
- "I wonder why..."
- "How do you think that happened?"
- "What do you know about...?"
- "How do you think we can find out?"
- "How many ways can you...?"
- "How do you think _____ and _____ are alike? How are they different?"
- "Can you think of a way to...?"

Good teaching involves observing what children do, knowing how and when to ask questions and make suggestions, and knowing when to say nothing.

## Responding to Each Child

Observe children to see what they are interested in exploring and to find out what they already know about a topic. As you observe children using materials or making observations, consider what you can do to challenge their thinking. Ask yourself,

- "What materials most interest the children?"

- "What questions should I ask?"

- "Are there problems that I can encourage children to solve?"

**Infants, toddlers, and twos** make discoveries every day. Your excitement about their discoveries will encourage these young scientists to continue to explore the world around them. Your responses will help children experience the pleasure, excitement, and sense of competence that come with exploration and discovery.

| Observe | Reflect | Respond |
|---|---|---|
| Jeremy crawls over to the low discovery shelf and pulls out the plastic container of large shells. He sits up and dumps them on the floor As he picks each one up, he shakes it and holds it to his ear. He puts one in his mouth but quickly takes it out. He spends quite a long time doing this. | Jeremy is using his senses to explore objects. *(Objective 11, Demonstrates positive approaches to learning; Objective 24, Uses scientific inquiry skills)* | Sit with Jeremy while he is playing with the shells. Describe what he is doing: "You are putting the shells back in the box."<br><br>Encourage him to dump them out again: "Can you take them out of the box? Oh, you dumped them *all* out. Now they are on the floor!"<br><br>Give him other safe natural objects to explore. Continue to describe what he is doing and ask questions: "That shell didn't taste very good, did it? Now, you're listening to the shell. Did it make a noise?" |

**Preschool children** want to know *what*, *why*, and *how* things happen. They explore the physical properties of things to figure out how they work. They feel feathers, pet animals, bounce and roll balls, run their hands through shaving cream, and spin tops. They seek answers to questions, for example, "How can I make the car go down the ramp faster?" and "Are the fish drinking the water in the tank?" They work with other children to explore materials and solve problems, and they like to share what they discover.

| Observe | Reflect | Respond |
|---|---|---|
| Nathan, Rosa, and Keisha cluster around the guinea pig cage. Nathan takes Murphy, the guinea pig, out and sits with him on his lap. | These three children play and work together well. *(Objective 2, Establishes and sustains positive relationships; Objective 25, Demonstrates knowledge of the characteristics of living things)* | Continue encouraging the children to work together: "Wow. You did two jobs. You fed Murphy, and you cleaned his cage." |
| Rosa says, "He hungry." She goes to the cupboard and fills a cup with guinea pig food. | Rosa speaks in two-word sentences in English. *(Objective 9, Uses spoken language to express thoughts and needs; Objective 38, Demonstrates progress in speaking English)* | Encourage them to help each other at cleanup time. Make a job chart and say, "Let's add feeding Murphy and cleaning his cage to our job chart. Those jobs are important." |
| "This cage needs to be cleaned," Keisha states in her best teacher-like voice. Rosa puts the food down and joins Keisha to clean the cage. | Keisha and Rosa know our FCC procedures and can complete a complex task. *(Objective 3, Participates cooperatively and constructively in group situations)* | Put out nonfiction books about guinea pigs and how to take care of other pets. Prompt, "Let's read *Dr. Friedman Helps Animals* to see if we should do other things to take care of Murphy." |

**School-age children** still benefit from exploring and experimenting with things that they can experience firsthand, but they are ready to think about more abstract concepts and to engage in more in-depth scientific thinking. While preschool children might make a daily weather chart that shows whether it was sunny, partly cloudy, rainy, hot, or cold, school-age children might learn the names of different types of clouds, types of storms, and how forecasters predict the weather. While preschool children might know that some eggs become chicks and some caterpillars become butterflies, school-age children generalize and understand that complex living things change and go through life cycles.

As you set up a discovery area, consider these characteristics of school-age children:

**They can think in abstract terms.** Talk with them about issues such as recycling and global warming. Encourage them to make predictions about the future.

**They are increasingly able to read and write.** Encourage them to read about scientific topics that interest them and to write descriptions of experiments they conduct. They can use their technological skills to document their learning in creative ways.

**They become systematic in their approach to problem solving.** Allow them to work on a problem and explore a number of possible alternatives. Help them think about the pros and cons of each possibility.

**They can analyze information.** Which brand of paper towel is *really* the strongest? Which can absorb the most water before it tears? School-age children can make predictions, devise and carry out safe experiments on their own, and form conclusions based on facts.

| Observe | Reflect | Respond |
|---|---|---|
| Tyrone has finished the dinosaur diorama that he made as an art project. He shows it to you and says, "I need to do some research about dinosaurs. If dinosaurs were so big and strong and ruled the world, what happened to them?" | Tyrone's interest in dinosaurs has made him curious about a big question: Why did the dinosaurs disappear? He did a lot of creative work with dinosaurs (making polymer clay figures and a diorama), and now he seems interested in learning more about them from a scientific point of view. | Encourage Tyrone to use books and the Internet to learn more about dinosaurs: "Tyrone, I have a book about dinosaurs that you're really going to like. It's a pop-up book by Robert Saboda and Matthew Reinhart. The pop-up dinosaurs will remind you of your diorama. It's full of interesting information." |

## Involving Children in a Study

One excellent way to support discovery for preschool and school-age children is through long-term studies. Studies are in-depth investigations of topics of interest to the particular children in your group. They support children's wonderful ability to become totally engaged in topics and activities that interest them, and they challenge children to extend their thinking to ever-higher levels. They are meaningful to children because they provide them with opportunities to gain information through direct observation and experimentation and then to link new ideas to what they already know. Chapter 3, "What Children Are Learning," outlines the steps for conducting a study and explains how to select an appropriate topic.

If you are just learning how to do a study, *The Creative Curriculum® Study Starters* can guide you through the process. *Study Starters* are step-by-step guides to project-based investigations in science and social studies. For each of 13 topics (boxes, ants, balls, clothes, flowers, buildings, exercise, wheels, trash and garbage, water pipes, rocks, chairs, and shadows), they explain how to begin a study, conduct investigations, and conclude the study. They also provide the background information you will need (in case, for example, you don't remember much about mass, momentum, gravity, energy, and friction from your science classes). They help you think about how to integrate content learning, give you sample investigations for children, and suggest ways to celebrate children's learning.

Studies are wonderful ways for children of different ages to be engaged in learning together, and you'll surely find yourself learning interesting ideas as well. You do not have to be limited to the *Study Starters* topics. *Study Starters* can help you become familiar with guiding a study, but the sky's the limit when it comes to selecting a topic—provided it is based on your children's interests, is meaningful to them and relevant to their lives, and can be investigated firsthand.

## Engaging All Children

All children make discoveries. Infants, toddlers, preschool children, and school-age children can all participate in a discovery activity in their own ways. Here's an example of what that might be like in your family child care home.

---

Tyrone (8 years) arrives after school one afternoon and announces, "We went on a hike over the weekend, and I found a lot of great rocks. Look at this one! My mother says it's mica. Look how I can peel the layers."

You smile and say, "That interesting. What else did you find on your hike?"

Tyrone empties an assortment of rocks on the discovery table. "Wow!" you say. "That's quite a collection! It must have been a long hike. I wonder what the other rocks are."

"Let's get a rock book," Tyrone says, "so I can look them up."

You respond, "Good idea. Tyrone, I used to collect rocks. I'll find my old collection so we can take a look at it, too."

The next day, you set your rock collection on the discovery table. Rosa (4 years) and Keisha (4 ½ years) begin sorting the rocks and placing them on the balance scale. You notice that they have sorted by size, so you prompt, "I wonder how else you could sort them." They continue to sort, using the magnifying glass to look at them and putting them into two piles based on whether or not they have flecks of color.

As you all head outdoors to the backyard, Keisha suggests, "Let's collect more rocks today." Outside, Jorge (2 ½ years), Nathan (3 years), and Rosa (4 years) join her in collecting rocks and putting them in grocery bags. Even Tamika (19 months) toddles over with a few rocks to put in a sack.

Tyrone is excited about your collection, the additional rocks gathered in the yard, and the fact that the other children share his interest. You sit with Tyrone, Rosa, Jorge, and Nathan and say, "You've been looking at rocks today. What do we know about rocks now?" You write their answers on chart paper: "Rocks are hard. Some rocks are big, and some are little. They are different colors. We have rocks in the backyard. Little rocks are called *pebbles*."

"Big rocks are called *boulders*," Tyrone adds. "Some people climb rocks, but I think that's scary."

"Is there anything else you want to know about rocks?" you ask.

Tyrone thinks for a moment and suggests some questions, "Where else can I find interesting rocks? How many different kinds of rocks are there, and what are they made of?"

"I have an idea for something we can do tomorrow to help us think about what rocks are made of," you say. "Let's leave our list of questions on the wall and add more as we think of them."

This scenario illustrates the following points:

- Children of different ages can explore natural materials found right in your own yard and neighborhood.

- Children have a lot of questions about the world. You can help them find the answers to their questions by finding out what they want to know, providing materials and resources, and setting up investigations.

- You can learn what children are interested in by listening to their questions and observing how they use materials.

- Open-ended questions extend children's learning.

- While learning science, children are also building their literacy and math skills and learning to work together.

# Partnering With Families

Families will be interested in knowing why you offer discovery experiences for young children. You can build your partnerships with families by using and sending home *LearningGames®* activities and by sharing the letter to families about discovery.

## LearningGames® for Discovery

### 12–24 months

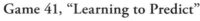

**Game 41, "Learning to Predict"**

Share with families the idea that children are born scientists. Children are curious about how things work and how they can make things happen. In this *LearningGames* activity, the child rolls a ball through a tube and finds—to her great surprise—that it comes out the other end! Playing this game again and again delights children again and again, and it helps them learn to anticipate what will happen. Changing the size of the ball or the angle of the tube will provide even more surprises. Show families how you keep a ball and tube handy for a bit of fun throughout the day.

### 24–36 months

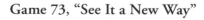

**Game 73, "See It a New Way"**

Keep plastic magnifying glasses available to children in your home and share with families how children use them to examine small objects and living things outdoors. Magnifying glasses enable children to see ordinary objects in a new way. Encourage families to talk about the differences the child is noticing, using words like *big* and *different*. Remind them to supervise closely when the child is handling tiny objects.

36–48 months

## Game 108, "Planting Together"

Perhaps you have a window garden or outdoor garden in your family child care home. Gardening is a great activity for families as well. It begins with planting seeds, but seeds take time to grow. Over time, families can have conversations about what plants need in order to grow (soil, light, and water); take pictures of the plants as they grow; and take turns caring for the plants. Working together on a project can be very rewarding for both parents and children.

---

48–60 months

## Game 154, "Inspect and Collect"

Encourage families to support their children's curiosity by noticing when their children pick up small objects, by talking about their discoveries, and by displaying their treasures. This *LearningGames* activity suggests ways to store and display collections, such as putting fragile items in the sections of an egg carton or putting hard items in water to make their colors brighter. When a child loses interest in one collection, she can explore a new one. Invite families to let their children bring collections to your program to share with other children and you.

---

[1] Mish, F. C., et al. (Eds.). (2003). *Merriam-Webster's collegiate dictionary* (11ᵗʰ ed.). Springfield, MA: Merriam-Webster, Inc.

# A Letter to Families About Discovery

Dear Families,

Young children are born scientists. They are curious about the world around them and have many questions. They ask, "Where did the puddle go? What do worms eat? How can I make my truck go faster? Do fish go to sleep?"

In my family child care program, I encourage all of the children to explore and investigate to find answers to their questions about the physical and natural world. Infants learn by using all of their senses. They want to know how things look, feel, taste, smell, and sound. Toddlers and twos experiment, trying to discover how things work, what things do, and what they can make happen. Preschool and school-age children observe, experiment, measure, solve problems, take things apart, and investigate living and nonliving things.

With appropriate support, children do what scientists do: ask questions, plan and conduct investigations, gather information, construct an explanation, and communicate findings. They learn important concepts as they study plants, animals, magnets, light, shadows, rainbows, the human body, how things move and change, and more. They learn how to solve problems together and how to communicate with others. When children are very interested in a topic, we spend a lot of time investigating it.

You don't need to be an expert to help your child learn about science. Science is all around us, from making bubbles in the bathtub to boiling water on the stove. Your own curiosity and your ability to ask questions will encourage children to make discoveries. Let your child know that you don't have all the answers but that you can find them together by observing, guessing, experimenting, looking things up, and conducting investigations. Get in the habit of wondering out loud: "I wonder how that ant can carry that big piece of food" or "I wonder why your shadow is sometimes small and sometimes big."

Your questions and statements support your child's scientific thinking skills. Here are some examples of prompts that extend your child's thinking:

- "What do you think will happen if...?"
- "I wonder why..."
- "How do you think we can find out...?"

Look for opportunities to promote your child's scientific thinking during everyday activities: playing with toys, taking a bath, helping to make dinner, or playing in the backyard. It's a good sign if your child is curious, wants to discover everything, asks lots of questions, and wants more answers!

Sincerely,

# Music and Movement

17

# Music and Movement

While Jeremy (8 months), Tamika (19 months), and Keisha (4 ½ years) play with toys on the living room floor, you play quiet background music. As you stack rings with Tamika, you notice that Jeremy is moving his body to the music. Catching your eye, he lifts his arms toward you and grunts. "Excuse me, Tamika," you say, "Will you play on your own for a minute? I think Jeremy's looking for a dance partner."

You get up, lift Jeremy in your arms, and start swaying to the music. Keisha joins you, saying, "I want to dance, too." You extend your left arm to Keisha, look at Tamika, and smile. She immediately stands up, takes Keisha's free hand, and all of you dance and sing along to the music.

Music affects our emotions. Like Jeremy, Tamika, and Keisha, most children are drawn to music. Sometimes it inspires us to move, and sometimes it helps us to be still. A lullaby calms a baby to sleep. If you play a march or other lively music, children will dance or stomp, trying to keep time with the beat. When you play a familiar song, children sing and hum along. Music is powerful, and it brings joy and beauty to our lives.

Music not only helps us express ideas and feelings, it also supports academic learning, particularly math. Music and movement experiences promote listening skills, language development, and physical strength and coordination. Children learn about patterns as they sing lyrics, play an instrument, and repeat actions. As they clap to the words and beat of a song, they learn about numbers and syllables. These are early math and reading skills.

Children engage in music and movement activities in five basic ways: listening, singing, moving to music, playing instruments, and imitating and representing music.

# Setting Up for Music and Movement

Music and movement experiences may occur wherever space permits. When the weather is good, take music and movement materials outdoors for experiences that are very different from indoor experiences.

## Choosing Materials and Props

### Listening and singing

The first and best exposure to music for babies is the human voice, talking and singing. Infants also hear other music: the tune that a mobile hanging over the changing table plays as it turns and the songs played by some toys.

Young children are captivated by musical toys. They endlessly open and close the parts of a busy box that make music start and stop. They turn the crank of a jack-in-the-box, laughing with delight each time the clown pops up.

As children get older, you will want to have a tape or CD player, or another device for playing musical recordings. Young children tend to prefer music and songs that have a strong rhythm, repetition, and nonsensical words and lyrics. They like music that evokes a mood, that suggests different movements, or that tells a story. The many wonderful recordings of music for young children range from traditional favorites to new songs. If you are unsure of which recordings to offer young children, remember that Raffi, Hap Palmer, Tom Glazer, and Pete Seeger have long been recognized for their talents. Provide soft furnishings for listening to music. Sofas and beanbag chairs are especially cozy for young listeners.

The music that appeals to preschool and school-age children includes the same classics with which you and generations before you grew up: "My Darling Clementine," "Kumbaya," "This Little Light of Mine," and so on. Some recommended musical artists are Ella Jenkins, Thomas Moore, Cathy Fink and Marcy Marxer, and Tom Hunter.

### Moving to music, and imitating and representing music

Many young children learn to connect music and movement as they push and pull toys that play songs and make other musical sounds. They push a toy lawnmower faster to make the music speed up and shake foam blocks to make bells jingle.

Fingerplays are particularly appealing to young children who feel an urge to move their hands to music. They delight in the repetitive language and simple story lines of fingerplays. "Itsy-Bitsy Spider" and "Where Is Thumbkin?" are fun and interesting.

Many children's storybooks support music and movement activities. Simms Taback's Caldecott award-winning book, *I Know an Old Lady Who Swallowed a Fly*, is a delightful version of the folk song. *Baby Beluga (Raffi Songs to Read)* is a picture book based on a popular song.

Many, many wonderful musical recordings were made specifically for preschoolers and school-age children. Many songs, like "Head, Shoulders, Knees, and Toes"; "The Mexican Hat Dance"; and "Hokey-Pokey" can be sung as line dances and musical games. To encourage creative movement, include props such as paper streamers, colorful scarves, large pieces of fabric, hats, clothes from various cultures, pom-poms, feather boas, kites, and so on.

## Playing instruments

Very young children like instruments that they may bang, ring, swish, and click:

- ankle bells
- drums
- xylophones
- pianos
- rattle
- shakers
- tambourine sticks
- maracas
- cymbals
- wood blocks

Make sure that anything with small objects inside or attached, such as a shaker or a bell, does not present a choking hazard. For a less expensive alternative to purchased instruments, you can turn pots and pans upside down, offer wooden spoons, and observe as children bang away, experimenting with different rhythms and sounds.

For older children, you will want to add items like these to your inventory of instruments:

- kazoos
- a keyboard
- a banjo
- a ukulele
- an autoharp
- rhythm sticks
- tone blocks
- tambourines
- triangles
- finger cymbals
- castanets
- melody bells
- rainsticks

### Supporting dual-language learners

Here are some ideas about supporting dual-language learners through music:

- Play music in the children's home languages.
- Encourage family members to record songs in their home languages so that you can play them during the day. This is a wonderful way to help children explore music and to stay connected to their families while they are with you. Playing lullabies sung by important adults in their lives soothes children during nap times.
- Remember that songs and fingerplays help children acquire languages. The catchy rhythm of songs often makes the lyrics easy to learn. Singing with a group also provides a safe environment for dual-language learners to use their emerging English skills.

You do not need to have everything suggested in order to provide a rich music program. If you find that having all of these instruments is too costly, just purchase a few select items, such as triangles, bells, and a xylophone. You can also make instruments. Try making drums from oatmeal boxes; cymbals from aluminum pie plates; and rattles from containers filled with buttons, acorns, or rice. Secure the openings firmly so the filling does not present a choking hazard.

Some older children want to practice the instruments they play at school. They usually have their instruments and sheet music with them, so they only need a place to practice and your support. Almost all older children like listening to poplar music and learning and practicing the latest dances. Other children may want to exercise to music. If the children in your program are eager to dance or exercise, provide space and appropriate music for them.

## Displaying Materials and Props

You can hang musical instruments or props like scarves and streamers on pegboard or clothes hooks. If you place the hooks at the children's shoulder level, they can reach these props on their own. Make silhouettes of the instruments or props from solidly colored contact paper and attach the cutouts beneath the hook where the item is hung. This enables children to clean up after themselves.

Make labels to identify tapes and CDs. Use pictures of children dancing, marching, resting, and so on, or use colors or symbols to identify types of music (show tunes, classical, folksongs, and so on). These can be taped to the ends of the storage containers so children can tell what is inside.

# Caring and Teaching

Think for a moment about a favorite song from your childhood. Where did you sing it? What were you doing? What made the song memorable? We remember musical experiences when they touch our emotions as well as our minds. Music is a language, a way to express thoughts and feelings and to tell stories. Equally important, music and movement help people form relationships with one another.

As a provider, you select music for children's enjoyment and for learning experiences. Your role is to promote children's development by giving them many opportunities to participate in music and movement activities, watch what they do, and then reinforce and extend their learning.

## Responding to Each Child

Children approach music and movement activities in ways that are characteristic of their ages and developmental levels. **For infants**, music can be a welcome part of everyday routines and activities. Your voice is their favorite music, even if you can't carry a tune! Play soft music for children at nap time and sing with them as you change their diapers. Promote children's attention and listening skills by playing music selectively and inviting a child or two to listen with you for a few minutes. Play music for short periods throughout the day, perhaps to set a tempo for gross motor activities or to influence a child's mood (for instance, to soothe an upset child).

Music is also a wonderful way to help children feel connected to their families while they are separated. Ask families about the songs they sing at home and the kinds of music they like. Learn the lullabies that a family sings at bedtime. As much as possible, include music from the children's home cultures and languages.

| Observe | Reflect | Respond |
|---------|---------|---------|
| As you sing, "Open, shut them. Open shut them. Give a little clap…," Jeremy watches you intently. He opens and closes his hands after you do and then claps them together. When you repeat the song, he follows your actions again and laughs. | Jeremy is carefully watching and imitating my actions. *(Objective 11, Demonstrates positive approaches to learning)*<br><br>Jeremy is amused by this finger play. *(Objective 35, Explores dance and movement concepts)* | Describe what you see Jeremy doing and provide more opportunities to act out simple songs: "Jeremy, you clapped your hands, just as the song says. You had a good time, following the directions in the song! Let's sing some more songs and clap to the music." |

**Toddlers and twos** pay attention to the sounds around them, and they might run to the window to listen to a chirping bird or a passing plane. They have learned to discriminate among many sounds and to identify their sources. They can match the sound *moo* to a picture of a cow and the sound *meow* to a picture of a cat.

Toddlers and twos can make almost anything into a musical instrument. They often experiment by shaking, tapping, banging, hitting, and pounding a variety of objects. They are learning songs that they particularly like and want to sing again and again. They hum and sing as they play, and they can sing some of the lyrics of familiar songs. They fill in words when you pause while you sing, just as they complete a sentence in a story, especially when the song includes rhyme and repetition. You may also hear them singing catchy jingles they hear on television and the radio. Encourage children to create their own songs. Sing along when you hear them singing a made-up song while putting their dolls to sleep. Encourage them to create new verses for their favorite songs.

As their fine and gross motor skills develop, children have more control over their bodies. This enables them to experiment with various kinds of movement. They especially enjoy participating in fingerplays and singing games. As children circle and fall during "Ring Around the Rosie" or jump enthusiastically when you play "The Bunny Hop," they are learning new concepts, language, social skills, and physical skills.

| Observe | Reflect | Respond |
|---|---|---|
| While most of the children are in the kitchen making fruit salad for lunch, Tamika toddles over to the cabinet, pulls out two pot lids, and bangs them together. Delighted by the sound, she starts hitting the lids together harder. The older children hold their ears, and Keisha protests, "Too much noise!" | Tamika has made cymbals out of pot lids. She is discovering that she can make musical sounds by banging the lids together. *(Objective 11, Demonstrates positive approaches to learning; Objective 34, Explores musical concepts and expression)*<br><br>I need to redirect Tamika so she doesn't disturb the other children. *(Objective 1, Regulates own emotions and behaviors)* | Talk about what she is doing and offer her a way to make music without disturbing others: "Tamika, you're making music with pot lids. That was a good idea! Unfortunately, your music is too loud for the other children. If you want to make music with the lids, you will need to wait until we go outside. If you want to make music now, try using this pot with a wooden spoon. It will make softer sounds." |

**Preschool children** enjoy listening to music in both group settings and by themselves, often using headphones. They are able to notice variations in musical selections, such as changes in tempo (fast or slow), pitch (high or low), and volume (loud or soft). They love to hear recordings of their own singing.

With the ability to match sounds and tones, children develop the ability to sing in tune. This pleases everyone, because preschoolers love to sing spontaneously as well as during planned activities. By age 3 or 4, children can typically keep time to a regular beat. They begin to adjust their body movements to changes in the music, responding to contrasts such as slow and fast tempos, or high and low pitches. They also learn to represent the motions of objects as well as people.

Even young preschoolers can use instruments. Although they may not match the rhythm of their instruments to their steps, they beat sticks while marching. Older preschoolers can play simple percussion or rhythm instruments, such as bongo drums, keeping the tempo of another instrument or a recording that is playing simultaneously.

| Observe | Reflect | Respond |
|---|---|---|
| Knowing that Nathan has excellent motor skills, you ask him whether he would like to join the older girls in moving to music like farm animals. He nods enthusiastically and starts galloping like a horse. | Knowing that Nathan has an Individualized Education Program because of articulation problems, you look for activities in which he can excel. He demonstrates strength and coordination of large muscles. *(Objective 4, Demonstrates traveling skills)* | Extend Nathan's strengths, applying the techniques that the special education teacher has shown you: "Nathan, you are an excellent horse! You gallop fast enough to be a racehorse! Will you say the word *gallop* with me?" |

**School-age children** will probably want to listen to music of their own choosing and with the privacy of headphones. They might also want to dance or exercise to music. Your role is to provide them with the space to do this and either the privacy or audience they prefer.

Some children will be exploring their talents for singing and for playing instruments. You want to support children's musical activities so that they can pursue their interests and refine their skills. Again, coordinate with the children's families to make sure they are practicing enough. Equally important, make sure children have opportunities to enjoy music.

| Observe | Reflect | Respond |
| --- | --- | --- |
| Tyrone arrived at FCC with lots of smiles and a brand-new MP3 player. "I can't wait to start downloading tunes," he announces. | Tyrone loves music, so having his own MP3 player is thrilling for him. I know from experience, though, that some of the music he likes uses language I don't want at my FCC program. If I don't act now, we're going to have a battle later. | Let Tyrone know the rules right away: "That's a beautiful player, Tyrone. Before you start loading your player with music, your parents and I need to discuss the types of music that you may play here. Today you may use the computer and start bookmarking sites that offer free music downloads." |

## Engaging Children of All Ages

Children enjoy music and movement experiences by themselves and with groups. Balancing the interests and skills of children of different developmental levels is one of a provider's greatest challenges. Here is an example of how you might approach a musical experience with a group:

After two days of heavy rain, the children are wound up from not playing outside. To work off their pent-up energy, you have been encouraging the children to move to music like different zoo animals, but they are becoming bored. You know that the children would probably love to march to music, but you don't think you have enough instruments for them. Eyeing the art supplies and some empty cereal boxes in your collection of recyclables, you come up with a solution. You ask, "Boys and girls, how would you like to form a marching band and parade around the house wearing costumes and playing instruments?"

The children chorus, "Yes!" and "¡Si"!

"Nathan (3 years), Rosa (4 years), and Keisha (4 ½ years), will you please help me put out the materials we'll need?" As you and the children set out the materials, you say what each type is called: *construction paper, feathers, paste, stapler, hole punch, yarn, rubber bands, oatmeal box, cereal box, pie weights, buttons, bottle caps, waxed paper, paintbrush, paint, paper towel tube, scissors.*

"Rosa, you and Nathan are in charge of costumes. You may use our dress-up clothes. You may also make a crown, put feathers on a hat, or make anything else you'd like."

"¡Que bueno! Me gustan los disfraces"! replies Rosa, grinning widely.

"Keisha, you, Jorge (2 ½ years), and I will make some instruments. We can make a kazoo, a shaker, and even a tambourine. If Tamika (19 months) and Jeremy (8 months) wake up from their naps, they will join us."

Everyone gets right to work. You show Keisha how to make a kazoo by painting a shortened paper towel tube, punching three holes in it, putting waxed paper around one end, and securing the waxed paper with a thick rubber band. Meanwhile, you guide Jorge through the process of making a tambourine. You ask him to help you hold the punch as you make holes along the edges of two paper plates. Then you show him how to put bottle caps between the plates. You also have him guide the yarn around the plates as you sew them together.

When the costumes, kazoo, and tambourine are ready for the marchers, Keisha still wants to make a shaker. She asks,

"What can I put in this oatmeal box to make noise?"

You suggest, "Why don't you experiment with what's on the table to see what works best. Do you think feathers will make good noisemakers? How about pie weights? Will buttons work?"

"Feathers are too feathery," Keisha responds. I'm going to try pie weights, because I know they make noise when I drop them." Gathering a handful, Keisha puts them in the empty oatmeal container. Much to her delight, they are easy to hear when she shakes them. "That's good!" she confirms.

"Okay, everyone," you announce. "While I put *Number March* on the CD player, pick out your costume and instrument and line up. Get ready for the best marching band this house has ever seen!"

---

This scenario illustrates several important points:

- Children of various ages can all participate in musical activities, but they approach the activity with varying skills.
- Dual-language learners (like Jorge and Rosa) and children with disabilities (like Nathan) and can all participate fully in music and movement experiences.
- You can expand your inventory of musical instruments by making simple ones.
- Making instruments gives children an opportunity to solve problems and experiment.
- Children need daily gross motor activities, and music encourages them to move.

# Partnering With Families

In addition to making instruments with the children in your program, you can involve family members during a workshop or open house. You can also share information with families by using and sending home *LearningGames®* activities and by sharing the letter to families about music and movement.

## LearningGames® for Music and Movement

### Birth–12 months

**Game 16, "Ride a Horsie"**

In this well-loved game, a baby sits on an adult's lap and goes for a rhythmic ride—up and down, up and down—as the adult recites, "Ride-a-horse, ride-a-horse, up and down." Soon the baby will laugh and kick his feet as he gets ready to be raised and lowered. He can predict what will happen next.

### 12–24 months

**Game 64, "Trying New Motions"**

In this *LearningGames®* activity, children try to move in different ways: sideways, backwards, or across a low bridge. Children will have fun crawling on their hands and knees with their mothers and fathers. This activity becomes even more fun when a familiar song encourages children to try moving another way. For example, everyone might sing, "If you're happy and you know it, turn around…"

### 24–36 months

**Game 98, "Run and Walk Together"**

Families can play this movement game outside. There are many ways to walk and run: slowly, quickly, backwards, sideways, galloping like a horse, or lumbering like an elephant. As families talk about each motion, they help their children learn words for actions and become aware of their bodies and how to move them. Share with families the motions and actions you are naming and practicing with children in your family child care home.

36–48 months

### Game 122, "Searching for Sounds"

Prompt children to listen to sounds around your house and encourage families to do so when they are at home. Explore objects throughout the house to see what sounds they make. Will it clang, clang, clang or drip, drip, drip? Create a musical instrument by pairing a pot and a wooden spoon.

---

48–60 months

### Game 158, "Syllable Jump"

Families may be surprised that children can learn language skills by moving their bodies. In this *LearningGames* activity, they help their children step or jump as the syllables of their names are spoken. Then children jump as they say or hear the syllables of other words, such as their last names, their siblings' names, or their favorite toys. This game helps children pay attention to the sounds and parts of words. Moving their bodies often helps young children learn. Show families the hopscotch boxes you have drawn for this game at your family child care home.

# A Letter to Families About Music and Movement

Dear Families,

We often sing and move creatively in our program. Singing and moving to music give children a chance to hear and appreciate different kinds of music, express their feelings and ideas, and practice new skills. The children love our daily time for singing together, and music helps them learn rules and procedures (such as for washing hands). Here are some of the things I do to encourage children to enjoy and participate in music and movement activities.

- We listen to different kinds and tempos of music.
- We make our own instruments.
- We move to music and dance to different rhythms.
- We sing and chant throughout the day. For example, we sing a cleanup song when it's time to put toys away.
- We use music to express our emotions and ideas.

You don't have to play an instrument or carry a tune to enjoy music with your child. Many of the toys you already have in your home probably make music. Discuss the sounds the toys make as you and your child play with them. Mimic the sounds and hum the tunes.

Take a few minutes to sit with your child to listen to some music. Remember that the music you share with your child doesn't have to be "kid's" music. Introduce your child to reggae, country, jazz, classical, rap, or any music you like.

Here are some more ideas for enjoying music and movement with your child:

- Children love songs and chants about what they are doing at the moment, especially when their names are used. While pushing your child on a swing, you might chant, "Swing high, swing low, [your child's name] feels the wind from head to toe."
- Songs and lullabies can calm a child at challenging times, for instance, during long car trips, while waiting in line, or when grocery shopping.
- Songs can ease your child into tasks like picking up toys, getting ready to go outside, undressing for a bath, and so on. You might try making up a chant to the tune of "Here We Go 'Round the Mulberry Bush." You can sing, "Soapy water fills the tub, fills the tub, fills the tub…" or "We put the toys on the shelf, on the shelf, on the shelf…"

Sharing music and movement with your child is a wonderful way to build a warm, loving relationship and to encourage lifelong exploration.

Sincerely,

# Cooking

# 18

# Cooking

You announce that, in response to the children's request, you bought strawberries for today's snack. "¡Que bueno! Fresas"! shouts Rosa (4 years), who has been talking about strawberries since she had them for dinner last week.

You hand Jorge (2 ½ years) a colander and head toward the kitchen, holding Jeremy in your arms and leading Tamika by the hand. As everyone approaches the kitchen table with the baskets of strawberries, you explain, "After you put the berries in the colander, we'll wash and hull them."

Rosa asks, "What's that?"

"Oh," you respond, "*hull* means that we take the leaves, the stem, and a tiny bit of the top off the strawberries before we serve them. We use a tool called a *huller*."

Eating and cooking are a basic part of life and of your family child care program. Children eat lunch and snacks in your program every day, and sometimes they also eat breakfast or dinner while in your care. When children help prepare meals and snacks, they participate in activities that are also meaningful to adults. During dramatic play, children pretend to cook and bake. In your kitchen, they have the opportunity really to do so. Participating in grown-up activities makes children feel competent.

Cooking is also a sensory experience, as anyone who has smelled baking bread knows. It is a creative process, and children have opportunities to make something important. At the same time, children learn healthy eating habits, setting a pattern for good nutrition.

In addition to the many other benefits, cooking is a hands-on laboratory for learning. As children follow directions on picture-based recipe cards, they develop literacy skills. They acquire new words, such as *hull*. They learn math as they measure ingredients, and they learn science when they observe bread rising or corn kernels popping. They learn social studies when they discover that different families eat different foods. Under your supervision, they learn about technology by using a microwave, a blender, or a mixer. They learn about the arts as they decorate the dining table.

# Setting Up for Cooking

Your kitchen is probably already equipped with the materials and equipment children need for cooking. However, you can make your kitchen more functional for the young cooks who will share the space with you. As much as possible, use unbreakable utensils and other tools because children lose their grips, drop things, or accidentally bang what they are using against hard surfaces. Children work well with soft rubberized handles, such as those on the Good Grips™ brand of cooking tools.

## Choosing Materials and Equipment

Cooking activities for infants involve seeing, tasting, smelling, listening, and touching. They don't need special utensils. Their eyes, ears, mouths, noses, and hands are the only tools required. A teaspoon of rice cereal is a taste and texture sensation for 4- to 6-month-old babies. By time an infant is 8 or 9 months old, you and the baby can take turns directing food to his mouth. You might wish to give an infant a cracker to nibble or a spoon to hold while you spoon cottage cheese to her mouth.

Older infants, toddlers, and twos can begin to participate in food-preparation activities, using safe tools such as wooden spoons, plastic mixing bowls, rubber spatulas, vegetable brushes, pastry brushes, spreaders, mashers, and cookie cutters.

Preschool and school-age children can use a wide range of utensils and tools. With your guidance, children can learn to use kitchen tools and appliances safely, so they can participate fully in cooking activities. Here is a list of cooking tools that you might want to introduce to children:

**Suggested Cooking Equipment**

### Measuring

| | | |
|---|---|---|
| plastic/metal measuring spoons | plastic/Pyrex® measuring cups for liquids | plastic/metal measuring cups for dry ingredients |
| pitchers | | |

### Baking/cooking

| | | |
|---|---|---|
| aluminum foil | griddle | pastry brush |
| biscuit/cookie cutters | loaf pan (metal and Pyrex®) | pie plates |
| cake pans (round or square, metal and Pyrex) | muffin tin and liners | plastic wrap |
| | nesting mixing bowls | rolling pin |
| cookie or jelly roll sheet | plastic mixing bowls of various sizes | saucepans with lids, including a double boiler |
| cooling rack | | |

## Gadgets/appliances

| | | |
|---|---|---|
| blender | hand mixer | soft-grip vegetable peelers |
| candy thermometer | hullers | |
| can openers | ice-cream freezer | ice cream or cookie dough scoop |
| graters | manual juicer (citrus reamer) | melon baller |
| | mortar and pestle | timer |

## Utensils

| | | |
|---|---|---|
| butter/table knives | large slotted spoon | sifter or strainer |
| eggbeater | potato masher or ricer | small and large rubber spatulas |
| funnel | pumpkin-carving knife (child-sized) | |
| chef's knives (sharp ones with soft-grip handles) | rubber scraper | soft-grip wire whisks |
| ladle | safety scissors or cooking shears | tongs |
| | | vegetable brush |
| | sandwich spreader | wooden spoons |

## Accessories

| | | |
|---|---|---|
| aprons | pastry bag with coupler and tips | potholders or oven mitts |
| wooden cutting boards | | trivets |

## Displaying Materials and Equipment

Look around your kitchen. Do you need to change anything to make it safer and more child-friendly? Here are some ideas:

- Store materials for children's use in one place, preferably in low cabinets and drawers so that children can reach them.

- Place all knives and sharp tools, such as cheese slicers, meat forks, meat thermometers, ice picks, and skewers, out of children's reach.

- If possible, set up a table for children that is no taller than the average child's waist. Position the table near an electrical outlet so you can use a blender, electric frying pan, or mixer when cooking with the children. You may want to use an electric frying pan or wok instead of cooking on the stovetop when children are involved. Small appliances are more manageable for young cooks and are easier for them to control.

- Display signs that teach kitchen safety and health, for example, posters about handwashing and using caution around a hot stove. These signs will remind children to practice safe and healthy behaviors when handling food.

- Have cleaning supplies, such as mops, sponges, and paper towels within the children's reach. The goal is for children to be able to clean up messes by themselves. Of course, cleansers must be kept out of the children's reach.

- Provide aprons or smocks for each child. Inexpensive ones can be fashioned from men's shirts or oilcloth tablecloths and fastened at the neck with VELCRO™.

# Caring and Teaching

When you cook with children, you are a leader, a facilitator, and a teacher. Your first responsibility is to make sure that the children will be safe. Nevertheless, accidents might occur despite your best efforts to prevent them. It is very important for you to know the recommended first-aid procedures for treating shocks, burns, and cuts.

## Keeping Children Safe and Healthy

Children need to be taught how to manage hot pots and pans, ovens, burners, and knives safely. Here are some safety guidelines:

To prevent shocks and burns:

- Keep tap water at no more than 110 degrees Fahrenheit.
- Use thick, dry potholders to handle hot pots, pans, and dishes. Pot grips made of silicone are highly recommended because they are both waterproof and heatproof.
- Always dry hands before plugging in appliances.
- Make sure that outlets are not overloaded and that unused outlets have safety caps.
- Use only wooden spoons in pots and pans because metal utensils get very hot.
- Keep potholders, aprons, and dish towels away from heating elements.
- When using a stovetop, turn pot handles toward the center of the stove.
- When lifting lids off hot pots and pans, lift the lid so that the inside of the lid faces the back of the stove. This directs the steam away from the cook.
- Have a fire extinguisher as well as a first-aid kit nearby—just in case you need them!
- Keep an open box of baking soda on the counter. If a cooking fire occurs, smother it with the baking soda, not water. If flames break out in an oven or microwave, shut the door and turn off the appliance.

To prevent cuts:

- Introduce children to butter knives before introducing chef's knives.
- Grip knives only by their handles.
- Keep knives sharpened. Dull knives are more dangerous.
- Place knives flat on a cutting board, not on the counter, when they are not in immediate use.
- Never cut food in your hand.
- Teach children to tuck their fingers into a "claw" when holding foods in place to cut them. That keeps fingertips out of harm's way.

In addition to the safety practices listed above, it is crucial for you to be aware of children's food allergies or intolerances. For example, it is not unusual for young children to be allergic to peanuts or to be lactose intolerant. Other common irritants to children are eggs (especially the whites), tree nuts such as pecans and walnuts, fish and shellfish, soy, and wheat. You also need to avoid foods that are potential choking hazards. Chapter 7, "Mealtimes," also addresses health and safety issues related to food.

## Responding to Each Child

Think about the ages of the children in your care and their ability to use cooking tools and appliances. While young **infants** will not be cooking, they can be included in the cooking experience by observing you and the older children from a high chair, your lap, or your backpack.

| Observe | Reflect | Respond |
|---|---|---|
| While making vanilla pudding at the kitchen table, Keisha and Rosa smile and wave at Jeremy, who is sitting nearby in his high chair. Jeremy smiles back and waves his arms toward them wildly. | Jeremy is interested in what the older children are doing and has been watching the girls intently. When they make friendly gestures toward him, he responds positively. *(Objective 2, Establishes and sustains positive relationships)* | Encourage Jeremy's interest in being with the girls by moving him closer to the action. Put a dab of pudding on his tray so he can be a part of the activity.<br><br>Describe what he is doing: "You saw Keisha and Rosa making pudding. Here's some for you to enjoy. Doesn't it feel nice and smooth?" |

**Toddlers** and especially **twos** can participate actively in food-preparation activities. For example, they can shake cinnamon on applesauce, mix cottage cheese and sour cream together, or dip banana chunks into yogurt. As you help them prepare food, observe them carefully so you will know how to respond. Help children talk about what they are doing by describing what you see and by asking them questions.

| Observe | Reflect | Respond |
|---|---|---|
| Jorge uses the circular cookie cutter to make cheese shapes. He pushes the cutter hard and then carefully lifts the extra cheese from around it. Picking up the circle of cheese, he says, "Look, ball! Mira". | Jorge is refining his small-muscle skills and learning to recognize shapes. *(Objective 7, Demonstrates fine motor strength and coordination; Objective 21, Explores and describes shapes and spatial relationships)* | Talk about the characteristics and names of different shapes: "Jorge, I see that you turned the square of cheese into a different shape! The square had straight sides. Then you used the cookie cutter to make a circle. It has curved edges like a ball." <br><br> Encourage Jorge to use the circular cutter on other foods, such as bread. Afterwards, introduce him to cutters of other shapes. |

Young **preschool children** can wrap aluminum foil around a potato, dredge chicken legs with flour, and learn to use basic cooking equipment such as a mortar and pestle or a rolling pin. Older preschool children are ready for more complicated tasks. For instance, they can peel carrots, decorate with a pastry bag, and use most electrical appliances with adult supervision. They can also be taught to use real knives safely.

By involving preschool children in cooking experiences, you can teach them a wide range of cooking skills. Experiences that involve safety risks (slicing, grating, and coring, for example) must be supervised carefully. While most preschool children can learn to master all of the skills listed below, some skills, such as cracking an egg into batter, may still be difficult for some.

Here are some cooking skills that preschool children can learn:

| | | |
|---|---|---|
| basting | kneading | rolling with hands |
| beating | marinating | rolling with a rolling pin |
| coring | mashing | |
| cracking eggs | measuring dry ingredients | scrubbing |
| cutting | | shaking |
| dicing | measuring liquids | shredding |
| dipping | melting | sifting |
| draining | mixing | slicing |
| dredging with flour or crumbs | peeling with fingers | spreading |
| | peeling with a vegetable peeler | squeezing |
| grating | | stirring |
| greasing | pitting | |
| grinding | pouring | |
| hulling | | |
| juicing | | |

As children master cooking techniques, help them focus their attention on what they are doing so they can learn from their experiences.

| Observe | Reflect | Respond |
|---|---|---|
| While making dough, Keisha finds that it is too sticky to roll out. She lifts up the rolling pin with pieces of dough on it and calls you over. "How can I make the dough less wet?" | Keisha has observed the sticky dough and figured out the cause of the problem. Now she needs to test possible solutions. *(Objective 11, Demonstrates positive approaches to learning; Objective 24, Uses scientific inquiry skills)* | Encourage her to solve the problem: "Keisha, you used strong observation skills to figure out why the dough won't roll out. You're right; it is too wet. How you can make it drier?"<br><br>When Keisha suggests using a paper towel, encourage her to try it and watch what happens. Afterwards, prompt, "Well, that sure didn't work very well, did it? There are pieces of towel in the dough, but you don't want them there. Let's try another approach. Think about what's in the dough. Which ingredients were wet, and which were dry? Maybe the dough will get drier if you add more dry ingredients. What do you think?" |

**School-age children** often regard cooking as a privilege of being older. They like the idea of helping themselves to snacks they make themselves. Some enjoy cooking as a hobby and want to learn how to decorate cakes, garnish platters, and make healthy main dishes. Others enjoy inventing their own recipes. If the older children show an interest in cooking or specific cooking skills, encourage their participation in cooking experiences. Provide them with lots of opportunities to refine their skills.

| Observe | Reflect | Respond |
|---|---|---|
| Tyrone is icing the cupcakes you made for Nathan's birthday, decorating them with swirls and colored sprinkles. | Tyrone is applying his artistic skills to cake decorating. You want to encourage this talent. | Tell Tyrone, "You've done an amazing job of decorating the cupcakes. You know, Tyrone, some of the world's best pastry chefs are men. If you'd like to try your hand at decorating, I'll get some STYROFOAM™ rounds that you can use to practice." |

## Using Recipe Cards

As preschool and school-age children master basic cooking techniques, they can begin to make snacks, meals, and treats. Participating in an activity that is often only for adults is very exciting to children. While there are many ways to approach cooking with your FCC children, we suggest eight steps that will contribute to successful cooking experiences.

1. **Select appropriate recipes.** Pick recipes that the children can follow with only minimal support from you. Consider children's interests, healthy food choices, other learning you want to promote, safety concerns, the cultural relevance of recipes, and the cost of the ingredients.

   Your first recipes should be your own family's favorites, recipes for foods that you are comfortable preparing. Next, ask the children's families. What are some of the children's favorite things to eat?

   If you're looking for a specific recipe but can't find one appropriate for young children, call your county U.S. Department of Agriculture extension agent for ideas. Several Web sites are devoted to cooking with children, such as Cooking with Kids (http://www.childrensrecipes.com/) and Star Chefs' Cooking With Kids with Lynn Fredericks (http://starchefs.com/kids/index.shtml).

   A number of cookbooks have great ideas for cooking with children. *Cup Cooking,* by Barbara Johnson Foote, and *Pretend Soup and Other Real Recipes,* by Mollie Katzen and Ann Hendrickson, are highly recommended. *The Cooking Book,* by Laura Colker, is specifically written for use in family child care homes and centers.

2. **Make simple recipe cards** that illustrate each step of the recipe. Use drawings and a few words to tell children what to do during each step. By linking the pictures to the written steps, preschool children gain a foundation for learning to read recipes. Here's what recipe cards should look like:

3. **Make sure that you have all of the necessary ingredients** on hand and in containers that the children can handle. For instance, rather than give children a 5- or 10-pound bag of flour, store the flour in a container that holds no more than six cups.

4. **Explain the recipe to the children before they try to follow it.** Discuss what to do for each step.

5. **Ensure that all of the children are engaged in doing something.** Not all of the children have to participate in the cooking activity, but all of them need to be actively involved in a purposeful experience, like reading, building with blocks nearby, or taking a nap.

6. **Help children think about the experience as they cook.** Begin by describing what you see them doing. "You've making a big pile of grated cheese! Look how the piece of cheese you're holding has gotten smaller." Encourage children to think and talk about their actions. "Why do you think the recipe says we have to grate the cheese rather than use slices like the ones we put in sandwiches?" Pose questions to help children think about their observations. "How does the grater shred the cheese into tiny pieces? Could you do the same thing with scissors?"

7. **Have the children put the food on dishes and encourage them to eat their creations.** Talk with them about the experience: "What did you most enjoy making?" "Which is your favorite food?" "What food on our plates will help us see well?"

8. **Include the children in the cleanup.** Cleaning up is the last step in the cooking process. Washing and drying cooking tools, wiping the table, sweeping the floor, composting scraps, and recycling are all tasks children can help with as part of a cooking experience.

## Engaging Children of All Ages

After putting Jeremy (8 months) in a backpack and Tamika (19 months) in the high chair, you assemble the other children in the kitchen for a planned cooking activity: making tacos. Yesterday you made recipe cards by using pictures to show the steps involved. Afterwards, you explained the recipe cards to Jorge (2 ½ years) and the preschool chefs.

To be ready for today's activity, you set all of the necessary utensils, equipment, and ingredients on the counter before the first child arrived. The recipe cards are ordered on a clothespin stand. Now you move everything to the table quickly. As the children put on smocks, you tie your apron and give Tamika some small chunks of cheese to nibble.

Keisha (4 ½ years) asked earlier whether she may grate the cheese. Under your careful supervision, she is scraping a large chunk of cheese across the grater, which you placed over waxed paper. You talk about what she is doing, "I see you're using your arm muscles to grate that cheese, Keisha. Is it hard work?"

"Not for me," she replies. "I'm a really strong kid."

"How did you get so strong?" you inquire.

"From playing outside and drinking my milk," she answers. After concentrating  intently on grating the cheese for 3 minutes or so, she begins to lose interest. "I'm finished with this stuff," she announces. "I don't want to cook anymore."

"Okay," you say. If you really don't want to make tacos anymore, you will have to do something else while I continue cooking with the others. Do you have a plan?" Keisha shakes her head *no*. "Well, you have some choices. The books and puzzles are out, and so are the LEGOS®. You may play with either of them. You may also write in your journal if you'd like."

As she walks into the living room, Keisha announces over her shoulder that she's going to play with the puzzles.

"We should start browning the hamburger while it's still easy for me to be here with you," you say. "Rosa (4 years), are you ready to put the hamburger meat into the electric frying pan? While Rosa and I brown the meat, Jorge and Nathan (3 years), you may tear the lettuce into pieces. I'm right here to help if you want me to."

This scenario illustrates several important points:

- Supervision is critical to having safe, successful cooking experiences.
- Children may leave the activity if they are bored, but they must get involved with other activities that do not require your direct support.
- Cooking activities are most successful when you plan. This means making recipe cards and having all ingredients and equipment ready.
- Children's cooking tasks must be age-appropriate.
- Include foods that are familiar to the children and that are among their favorites.

# Partnering With Families

Cooking activities can be a strong link between your program and the children's families. You can build your partnerships with families by using and sending home *LearningGames®* activities and by sharing the letter to families about cooking.

## *LearningGames®* for Cooking

### Birth–12 months

### Game 34, "Making Useful Choices"

Of course, young babies aren't actually involved in "cooking," but every meal is an opportunity for them to see, touch, smell, feel, and sometimes listen to new foods. An older infant may enjoy playing this *LearningGames* activity. Encourage families to invite their child to choose the appropriate tool: "It's time to eat. Would you like to use a spoon or a lid?" Ask families to think of other ways to prompt their children to make simple choices, just as you prompt the children.

### 12–24 months

### Game 59, "Beginning to Share"

Children this age do not know how to take turns, divide snacks, or give up toys they want to use. Encourage families to help their child practice sharing with others by giving him two of something and telling him that one is for him and the other is for someone else: "This cracker is for you, and this one is for Daddy. Will you please give it to him?" You can also use this simple technique in your program to help very young children begin to share.

24–36 months

### Game 100, "I See Something That Is..."

Encourage families to play this game while they are cooking and eating dinner. It's a guessing game in which they give two hints so the child can identify an object. For example, a parent might describe a plate by saying, "I spy something yellow. You put food on it." A child might guess, "Carrot" if her grandmother hints, "I spy something orange, and we're eating it for dinner." Play this game when parents come to pick up their children at the end of the day: "I see something you wear on your head. Don't forget to take it home!"

36–48 months

### Game 121, "See and Show"

In this activity, family members show their child how to do something and then encourage the child to explain the process to someone else. A simple cooking activity, such as making a celery snack, works well for this. Remind the family to organize the instructions in three main parts, for example, "Wash the celery. Dry the celery. Spread the cheese." Encourage children to use words to explain what comes first, next, and last. This involves important thinking and language skills.

48–60 months

### Game 177, "Today I Can"

Cooking involves many different skills that children can learn. Four-year-olds can squeeze a lemon, spread apple butter, crack an egg, cut a carrot, flip a pancake, knead bread, mix and roll out dough, pour milk—and the list goes on. Encourage families to select several skills for their child to learn and to help their child remember and practice the skills he has learned. An *I Can Cook* picture book is a fun way to help the child remember. At pickup time, encourage children to tell their families what they did in your FCC home during the day.

# A Letter to Families About Cooking

Dear Families,

Cooking is an important part of my program, just as it is in your home. When they cook, children have opportunities to learn about nutrition, to be creative, and to prepare their own healthy meals and snacks. Children learn a lot of academic skills, too. When children follow picture recipe cards, they begin to develop early reading skills. Measuring ingredients are math lessons. Whipping egg whites into meringue and melting cheese under a broiler are lessons in science.

Cooking experiences are very meaningful to children. In their dramatic play, children often pretend to be grown-ups, shopping for groceries, preparing food, and serving meals in homes and restaurants. They also read and sing about food. By actually cooking, children share an experience that is also important to adults. Do you have some favorite family recipes that you would like to share with us? We'd love it, too, if you could visit and cook with us once in a while.

When children cook, we talk a lot about what they are doing and why. I ask them to become scientists, to observe, for example, what happens as we combine ingredients and change their temperatures. We make predictions and experiment to find out how much we should fill a muffin tin so that the batter doesn't overflow.

Here are some suggestions for cooking with your child at home:

Think about ways to involve your child in the cooking that you do ordinarily. It may take extra time and be messier than if you cooked alone, but there are many rewards. Your child will be learning literacy, math, and science skills just by helping you. In addition, cooking sets the stage for lifelong healthy eating habits. When children have a hand in preparing their meals, they are more interested in what they eat and are more willing to try new foods.

Start by giving your child simple tasks like stirring batter, squeezing lemons, adding spices, and shaping meatballs or dough. Discuss what you are doing together while cooking. Ask questions such as these:

- What happened to the dry ingredients when we added the milk?
- How did you get the lumps out of the batter?
- Why do you suppose the recipe says to fill the batter only halfway up the pans?
- What was your favorite part of making muffins?

The beauty of cooking with your child is that your child is learning skills and having fun at the same time as you are attending to a household chore. What could be better than that?

Sincerely,

# Computers

# Computers

---

While working with a group of children who are putting puzzles together on the dining room table, Keisha (4 ½ years) comes over to ask, "May I use the computer now? Once Tyrone gets here, I'll never get a turn!"

You respond, "I know that it seems like Tyrone is always on the computer, but remember that he uses it to do his homework. You may certainly use the computer now. What would you like to do?"

Keisha explains, "I want to see the pictures from our trip to the bakery."

You offer, "I'll show you how to find them on the computer. If you want, we can print them and make a book about our trip."

Keisha exclaims, "Oh, yes! That's exactly what I want to do!"

---

Computers are increasingly a part of everyday life, as vital as telephones and nearly as common as televisions. They give us access to important information, help us keep in touch with others, provide entertainment, and even help us produce art and music. They introduce new cultures, people, and ideas to us.

Although 31 percent of children under age 3 have spent time at a computer,[1] that is not appropriate for very young children. Simply put, children under age 3 should not use a computer. Babies, toddlers, and twos need to master active skills like crawling, walking, talking, and making friends. They do not need to sit at a computer.

Older children, on the other hand, can benefit from computer activities. Much of what they learned as toddlers and twos, such as understanding colors, shapes, and sizes and learning to categorize, solve problems, create patterns, and so on can be reinforced by computer programs. Indeed, one of the best aspects of appropriate computer activities is that they help children learn to think abstractly. Some children's software introduces them to the arts and enables them to express themselves. Computers can help children with disabilities by supporting their self-confidence, controlling their environments, and promoting gains in language development.[2] Dual-language learners benefit from some of the computer software that uses two or more languages.

# Setting Up Computers

If you have a home computer, you must decide whether to make it available to the children in your program. If so, it should be located where you can supervise the children easily while they use it. When you set it up, keep several things in mind:[3]

**To keep the area safe, use a power strip** for plugging in the computer and any related equipment, such as a printer or scanner. Screw the power strip to the underside of the computer table or to a table leg where the children will not see it. Group the wires together with twist ties and, if necessary, fasten a hook to the bottom of the table to keep the wires out of reach. You need to be sure that the wires do not present a safety hazard, especially if you care for crawling babies.

**Position the computer monitor** so that the screen is directly in front of where children sit. Experts warn that bending the neck back to look at the screen leads to joint pain. Eyestrain can be avoided by placing children's chairs about a foot from the screen. To reduce glare, place the computer monitor parallel to a window. If users are right-handed, lamps should be placed to the left. Left-handed users need lighting from the right.

**Children should be able to use the keyboard and mouse with their wrists held straight.** They should be close enough to keep their elbows bent and their upper arms relaxed. This helps prevent carpal tunnel syndrome. The mouse should be within an arm's reach of the keyboard.

**Use an adjustable keyboard tray and a pneumatic chair.** This is especially important if the computer will be used by members of your family as well as the FCC children. Working with the computer at an appropriate height prevents stress-related disorders for users of every age. Also, because young children often work well in pairs, try to have two chairs of appropriate height at the computer table or desk.

## Choosing Software

Perhaps your biggest challenge will be to select software and identify Internet sites that are appropriate for your preschool and school-age children. The task can be daunting. In the 25 years since personal computers first appeared, over 12,000 pieces of software and Internet sites have been developed specifically for young children.[4]

While some software offers children exciting choices and experiences, other programs are merely a watered-down version of those developed for older children or an electronic version of worksheets. Flashy animation, bright colors, and interesting sounds are not enough to make software appropriate. In addition, there is a gender bias toward featuring male characters. Many are needlessly violent, too.

Even though the cost of software keeps dropping, investing in it can still be expensive. You do not want to waste your money (and the children's effort) on bad software. How do you weed through the seemingly endless number of choices? Here are some thoughts:

**Limit your software purchases.** Invest in only a limited number of high-quality selections, just as you do when buying children's books. Children tend to get more out of computer experiences when they explore a program's options in depth, rather than jump from one program to another. As children develop skills, they learn to use a program in different ways or at more advanced levels.

**Consult software experts.** Fortunately, these resources offer excellent reviews:

- *Children's Technology Review*™ (http://www.childrenssoftware.com/aboutcsr.html) Active Learning Associates, which publishes this product, is the premier reviewer of children's software. For a monthly fee, subscribers receive a magazine (either in print or online) that discusses the latest trends and 50 or more noteworthy products, including children's Web sites, video games, educational software products, and interactive DVDs. There is also a searchable database (Children's Software Finder™) of over 8,200 product reviews. The software is reviewed not just by experts but by children of the age for which the software is targeted.

- *Computing With Kids* (http://www.computingwithkids.com/default.asp) For a subscription fee, this site provides readers with weekly reviews of software, video games, Web sites, and "smart" toys. There is also a searchable database and access to top picks and relevant articles. Reviews are conducted by professionals in the field and sometimes by children.

- *SuperKids Educational Software Review* (www.superkids.com) This Web site provides free reviews of educational software and an index that can be searched by the software title and publisher. Like *Children's Technology Review*, each piece of software is reviewed by teams composed of teachers, parents, and children.

**Become your own software expert.** You need to know what you to look for when you are researching software. To help you evaluate software, a checklist is included in the appendix of this book.

**Consult with others.** Ask the children's family members, your local librarian, fellow providers, and other trusted resources for their ideas. One caution, though: Copyright laws prohibit you from copying software that you borrow or buy.

**Look for discounted software.** You can sometimes pick up software CDs at yard sales or dollar stores. Also, if you do not mind using earlier versions of newly-released software, you can frequently find unused CDs for sale on sites such as eBay®.

## Choosing Web Sites

The Internet has changed approaches to education. Even preschool children can benefit from the rich array of resources. However, the sheer number of sites can make it seem unmanageable. Like the quality of software, the quality of Web sites varies widely. Many, many sites are inappropriate for young learners.

Think about the Internet as you do children's software, and guide children's use of the sites from which they can benefit. Children should never use Web sites without your approval and supervision. The checklist included in the appendix to help you evaluate software will also assist you in judging the appropriateness of Internet sites. In addition, *Children's Technology Review*, *Computing With Kids*, and *SuperKids Educational Software Review* offer reviews of children's Web sites.

If you give school-age children access to your computer, it is vital that you consult with the children's families and install whatever parental controls they and you think are necessary. While you want children to enjoy their computer time, you need to be sure that they are safe.

Despite some drawbacks of the Internet, it offers wonderful online opportunities for children. They can explore the world with National Geographic, join book clubs, learn about cooking, post their photography, and publish their own poetry and stories. When computers are used wisely, they are powerful learning tools.

## Displaying Software

If you load software selections on the computer, you do not need to consider additional ways to display them for the children. However, if you do not want to take up space in your computer's memory by preloading programs or if you borrow software from a library or another source, you'll want to display the software CDs near the computer. Remember that CDs need to be handled carefully. They should be stored in CD pockets or jewel cases. The picture labels on the cases and the CD, itself, help children identify those they want to use.

# Caring and Teaching

The way you support children's use of computers will influence whether their experiences are meaningful or a waste of time. When children use the computer, you want to be sure that they are learning new skills and information, solving problems, doing research, expressing themselves, and having fun.

Even if children already use computers at their homes and schools, they need to learn about the one they will be using in your home. Sit at the computer with the children who will be using it and show them how your computer operates. Here are some of the things you will want the children to know:

- to hold a CD-ROM or DVD at the edges
- how to insert a CD or DVD into the disk drive
- the location of the keys that operate the program
- how to operate the mouse (or trackball) to move or point to items on the screen
- what happens when they click on the icons
- how to advance through the program
- sounds that indicate that the printer is working
- how to exit the program

If you have school-age children in your program, consider asking them to tutor the younger children. The older children will enjoy being looked to as computer experts, and the younger children will love being in their company.

## Responding to Each Child

Most **preschool children** are attracted to computers. They see adolescents and adults enjoying computers, and they want to use them, too. To be able to do what teenagers and adults do makes children feel grown-up in a way they seldom experience.

Many preschool children enjoy being at the computer so much that they want to spend entire days there. While children should have many choices about what to explore in depth, you do not want them to use the computer to the exclusion of other activities. Think about limiting their use to, say, an hour a day. Then encourage them to explore their interests through other activities. For example, if a child has been using the computer to read about spaceships, suggest that she build one with cardboard. If a child has been experimenting with musical tones online, suggest that he try what he learned by playing the xylophone.

Computers can support children's learning in many ways. At the same time that children are refining their small-muscle skills and perfecting their eye–hand coordination, they can learn many other skills and academic content. Programs like *JumpStart Advanced Premium Preschool* (by Knowledge Adventure) and Internet sites like http://www.gamequarium.com/junior.html introduce science and math concepts.

By exploring Web sites like http://www.enchantedlearning.com/geography, children can learn about geography, maps, and people in other lands and cultures. Children can learn about storytelling and other aspects of language with programs like *Sammy's Sticker House* (by Riverdeep). They can draw and paint by using drawing programs like *KidPix Studio Deluxe 4* (by Broderbund). They can learn about tone, pitch, and musical compositions, and they can sing along to their favorite songs with software like *Horace Hopper's Musical Adventures* (by Greenwood Studios). Children can edit photographs for a PowerPoint slideshow, read along with recordings of their favorite storybooks (http://www.storylineonline.net/), and send e-mail to children around the world.

As with all learning, children follow a developmental progression in their computer use. One of the most important ways to encourage preschool children to explore computers is to talk with them about their experiences. Indeed, computer time can and should be extremely social. Encourage two children to work at the computer together. That way they can decide how to work through a program together, support each other, and learn from each other.

Talk with children to help them think about what they are doing and why. As a first step, describe what you see children doing. Your descriptions let children know you are interested in their work and have confidence in their ability to use computers. Then ask questions to find out what they are thinking and to promote their development of process skills like problem solving, reasoning, making connections, communicating, and representing what they know.

| Observe | Reflect | Respond |
|---|---|---|
| While using *KidPix,* Keisha "paints" a picture of a fire truck. She then calls Jorge over to the computer. "Look, Jorge. I painted a picture of a truck that looks just like the one you brought from home. Watch me drive it off the screen!" | Keisha is using the arts to represent her ideas. *(Objective 33, Explores the visual arts)* <br><br> She is also learning to use particular software to draw. *(Objective 14, Uses symbols and images to represent something not present; Objective 28, Uses tools and other technology to perform tasks)* | Comment on what you see Keisha doing and ask open-ended questions that will extend her skills: "The truck you drew on the computer is the same color and shape as Jorge's truck. You can even make it move! That's amazing! How can you make your computer drawing look even more like Jorge's truck?" |

**School-age children** might already be adept at using the computer. According to the 2000 Census, 90 percent of school-age children use computers regularly.[5] Indeed, more school-age children use computers than adults do![6]

Once you find out how much time families want their children to spend on the computer and what activities are acceptable to them, you will have endless opportunities to work with school-age children on the projects they choose. They will probably spend some of their time at FCC on homework. The computer is a valuable tool for research and writing. Moreover, useful reference materials for students are available online, including dictionaries, encyclopedias, and style manuals.

Children can use computers to communicate with peers and check in with family members. They can also pursue their passions online by researching ideas, downloading free music, publishing their poetry, discussing books and ideas, simulating the construction of buildings, and sharing their creations. Under your supervision, children can participate actively in a community of worldwide learners.

One more point: Remember to enlist school-age children as mentors for preschoolers. Don't be surprised if they are able to give you computer advice as well! Take advantage of their knowledge and hone your own skills.

| Observe | Reflect | Respond |
|---|---|---|
| For several days, Tyrone has been working on a poem that was originally part of a school project. After turning it in, he has continued working with the poem on the computer, trying to make it even better. | Tyrone is very interested in writing poetry. I want to encourage this ability and his confidence about his work. | Comment on Tyrone's work and offer support: "Tyrone, you are certainly dedicated to writing your poem. What do you think about publishing it online where other children can see it? I found "The Poetry Zone," a site where children your age share their poems. Here's the Internet address." |

## Engaging Children of Different Ages

While computer activities should only be for preschool and school-age children, several children will often want to use the computer at the same time. That is what happens in the following scenario.

After her afternoon nap, Rosa (4 years) asks you whether she may work at the computer. The children have been writing to their friends at Mrs. Cawley's family child care home, and Rosa wants to know if there are any new e-mail messages from them. You sit with Rosa and show her how to retrieve messages. "Oh, look, Rosa!" you exclaim, "The children scanned a drawing they made for us. Let's download and print it!"

Hearing your conversation, Keisha (4 ½ years) puts down the book she was leafing through and pulls a chair next to Rosa's. "I want to see it," Keisha says excitedly.

As the drawing comes out of the printer, Nathan (3 years) and Jorge (2 ½ years) scurry over, too. You invite the children's ideas by prompting, "Look at what our friends made for us. What should we send back to them?"

"Let's send them one of our drawings," Keisha suggests.

"That's a great idea," you agree. "However, we don't have a scanner to copy a picture onto the computer. We can take a photograph of all of us and send that, though. What do you think?" Everyone agrees with the idea.

While you are taking the photo, Tyrone (8 years) arrives from school. He checks in with you and helps himself to a snack of vegetables and yogurt dip. Pacing near the computer rather impatiently, he says, "I have to do my homework. When will you be through?"

"Soon," the girls call out in unison.

You respond, "Tyrone, will you please help us send our photo as an e-mail attachment? Then the computer will be all yours."

This scenario illustrates several important points about children's use of the computer:

- It can be a very popular tool.

- There are many uses for the computer, for example, sending and receiving e-mail; downloading, organizing, and editing photos; and working on homework.

- Computer experiences can be very social; preschoolers can benefit from working in pairs.

- Children with different levels of skill can all have successful experiences on the computer.

- Children can teach themselves to use some software programs, and they learn to use other programs by being tutored.

- It is important for adults to supervise what children are doing on the computer.

Children can have rewarding experiences if computer use is planned and monitored thoughtfully. As noted above, planning involves the children's families. The letter that follows can be used to communicate with families about the use of computers in your program.

---

[1] Kaiser Family Foundation. (2003). *Young children spending time with computers and televisions.* Washington, DC: Author.

[2] Hutinger, P. L., & Johanson, J. (2000). Implementing and maintaining an effective early childhood comprehensive technology system. *Topics in Early Childhood Special Education, 20*(3), 159–173.

[3] Canada Safety Council. (January 2006). *Ergonomics for kids.* Safety Canada Online, XLX(1). Retrieved February 6, 2009, from http://www.safety-council.org/news/sc/2006/January.html

[4] Active Learning Associates. (2008). *Children's Technology Review*™. Retrieved February 6, 2009, from http://www.childrenssoftware.com

[5] U.S. Census Bureau. (September 6, 2001). *U.S. Department of Commerce News.*[Press release; Electronic version]. Retrieved February 6, 2009, from http://www.census.gov/Press-Release/www/2001/cb01-147.html

[6] DeBell, M., and Chapman, C. (2003). *Computer and Internet use by children and adolescents in the United States, 2001* (NCES 2004–014). Washington, DC: U.S. Department of Education, National Center for Education Statistics.

# A Letter to Families About Computers

Dear Families,

I am delighted to have a computer in my program to use with children aged 3 and older. As I'm sure you are aware, computers can be amazing learning tools when used appropriately. I want to work closely with you to ensure that your child's computer experiences are positive. I need to know how long you'd like your child to use the computer at one sitting and what types of software and Internet sites your child may use.

These are my goals for children's computer use:

- being comfortable with computer technology
- developing reading and writing skills
- learning math skills and understanding math concepts
- expressing themselves creatively
- learning to solve problems and find information

I encourage children to work at the computer in pairs. This helps them learn from each other and supports their social skills. While children are working at the computer, I ask them questions to help them think about what they're doing. For example, I might ask,

"Why did you choose this program?"

"How can you send a copy of your computer painting to your grandparents?"

"What would you like to do with the printouts you made today?"

By interacting with the children, I encourage their development and learning and help them prepare for a future in which they will need to know how to work with computers.

You may or may not have a computer at home. It is certainly not necessary for you to have one for your child to benefit from using the computer at my family child care program. If you do have a home computer and would like to know more about using it with your child, please ask. I will be glad to assist you, including sharing information about appropriate programs and Web sites.

By working together as a team, we can help your child have positive, meaningful experiences with the computer.

Sincerely,

# Outdoors

**20**

# Outdoors

"¡Mira, mira! Look! Snow!" exclaims Rosa (4 years), pointing out the window. Keisha (4 ½ years), Tyrone (8 years), Nathan (3 years), and Jorge (2 ½ years) run to the window to watch large flakes coming down.

"Oh, boy! I bet I won't have school tomorrow," predicts Tyrone, jumping up and down.

"Go out?" asks Nathan.

"Why not?" you respond. "Let's get our coats, hats, boots, and mittens on and go out in the snow."

After getting the older children to help you dress Jeremy (8 months) and Tamika (19 months), you take the children into the yard. "Wow!" exclaims Keisha, looking at a large snowflake on her jacket. "This snowflake looks like a star." Jorge and Nathan trot over to look at her snowflake. Soon all of the children are holding out their arms to catch the "starflakes."

Playing outdoors every day is essential for children's health and well-being as well as for yours! The outdoors offers an entirely different environment for children to explore: more open space in which to run and stretch, different equipment and landscapes to master, wildlife to marvel at, and fresh air and weather to experience. Nowhere else can children feel the warmth of the sun on their backs, watch a butterfly land on a flower, or dig in the dirt. The outdoors is filled with adventures and wonders.

Too many children today are not getting opportunities to play freely outdoors, where they can stretch and exercise their large muscles by running, jumping, climbing, and swinging. We are seeing an alarming increase in childhood obesity in the United States, due in part to the fact that children are not getting the benefits of active, outdoor play. Your commitment to taking children outdoors every day and encouraging their active play and exploration supports their physical development and nurtures their appreciation of nature.

# Setting Up for Outdoor Play

Outdoor environments for family child care programs range from the convenience of an easily accessed and protected yard around a house or an apartment building to a public playground to which the provider must walk with all of the children. You may have lots of grass, trees, and equipment designed for children to play on, or your space may be limited, perhaps just asphalt. No matter what kind of space you have, you can make outdoor time fun and safe for children.

## Keeping Children Safe and Healthly

Whenever you go outdoors, children's health and safety is always a primary consideration. Here are some factors to keep in mind, whether the children play in your own yard, another provider's yard, or at a public playground:

**Supervision**—Watching and being prepared to interact are the primary ways to keep children of all ages safe and healthy outdoors. Because you are usually the only adult, try to minimize the need to go indoors to take a child to the toilet or retrieve materials. Planning makes that easier.

**The layout**—The area where children play should be fenced and without protruding wires or nails. Children who are not yet mobile need to be protected from being bumped by children who are already crawling, walking, and running.

**Developmentally appropriate equipment**—Equipment should be designed to match the sizes and skills of the children in your care. A general rule for equipment height is one foot for every year of a child's age. For example, a 2-year-old should use equipment that is no higher than 2 feet from the ground. Swings, slides, see-saws, and climbing equipment should be firmly anchored to the ground. An adult should not be able to make a structure wobble or tip.

**Shock-absorbent materials**—Any surface higher than 18–24 inches should be surrounded by shock-absorbent material that meets Consumer Product Safety Commission guidelines. There should be a 6-foot fall zone around the equipment. Be cautious about material that children might choke on, such as pea gravel or small wood chips.

**Taking children on walks**—Make sure you have what you need to keep children safe when you take them on walks in the neighborhood or on field trips.

- Keep a backpack or tote bag supplied with a first-aid kit, diapers, hand sanitizer, wipes, water, snacks, and plastic bags.
- Bring a charged cell phone with you and contact information for each family.
- Have each children wear a tag with your name and phone number in case he or she wanders away from you.

**First-aid supplies**—Always keep two well-stocked first-aid kits available: one for your home and one to take on walks or field trips. According to National Association for Family Child Care (NAFCC) Accreditation Standard (4.10), each kit should include first-aid instructions, disposable nonporous gloves, soap and water or hydrogen peroxide, tweezers, bandage tape, sterile gauze, scissors, and a baby-safe thermometer.[1]

**Protection from too much sun**—In hot weather, sun hats, long-sleeved shirts, and pants provide sun protection. Families must provide sunscreen and written permission for you to use it on their child. Be sure to offer children extra water on hot days. To create shady places, set up large umbrellas, drape a sheet from a fence, put up a tent, or use an awning.

**Weather considerations**—As long as children are dressed properly, there is no reason to keep children indoors on hot or cold days. You can adjust your schedule to accommodate changes in the weather. For example, on a nice spring day or after the first snowfall, you may want to extend the time outdoors. On a cold and windy day, you may want to have shorter periods outdoors. Keep extra mittens, hats, and boots on hand. When the temperature is below freezing, teach children how to stay safe on metal structures such as climbing equipment or slides. Children's tongues can freeze to metal structures. Tell children not to move but to try to yell for help if this ever happens. Keep warm water available in a thermos to pour on the child's tongue to loosen it.

**Allergies**—You may have a child in your program who is highly allergic to insect bites or stings. Allergic reactions can become life-threatening situations unless you know exactly what to do. Keep a treatment kit readily available and always carry a cell phone while you are away from home so you can call 911.

**Nontoxic landscapes**—Check for poisonous plants, such as poison ivy, poison oak, elephant ears, mushrooms, and lilies of the valley. Be on the lookout for fire ants, spiders, and snakes. Check with your regional Poison Control Center or Cooperative Extension Service for complete information.

**Water safety**—According to *Caring for Our Children: National Health and Safety Performance Standards*, drowning is the third-leading unintentional injury of children younger than age 5.[2] In some states, it is the leading cause of death. To prevent drowning, outside play areas should not include unsupervised swimming and wading pools, ditches, canals, excavations in which water can collect, fish ponds, and other bodies of water.

**Minimizing conflicts**—You can reduce hitting, pushing, and biting incidents by offering plenty of interesting things to do. Provide duplicates of favorite outdoor toys such as balls, buckets, shovels, and riding toys. Be alert and ready to step in when necessary.

**Monitoring and Maintenance**[3]

Check daily for the following hazards and eliminate any problems:

- broken glass, needles, trash, and other hazardous materials such as animal feces, garden chemicals, and paint
- visible cracking, bending, warping, rusting, or splintering of equipment
- worn swing hangers and chains
- missing, damaged, or loose swing seats
- broken supports or anchors
- cement support footings that are exposed, cracked, or loose in the ground
- accessible sharp edges or points
- protruding bolt ends that have lost caps or covers
- loose bolts, nuts, and screws that require tightening
- splintered, cracked, or otherwise deteriorating wood
- broken or missing rails, steps, rungs, or seats
- hard surfaces, especially under swings and slides, where shock-absorbent materials have shifted
- chipped or peeling paint

## Creating Outdoor Structures

If you have enough room in your yard, you can create play structures for children. Here are some ideas:

**Natural materials**—Find out about nearby places (for example, a farm or gardening center) where you can get some bales of hay for the yard. If you keep them covered and protected from rain and snow, they will last a long time. Other natural materials you can bring are low tree stumps, driftwood logs (check for splinters), and large smooth stones.

**A garden**—You do not need to have a plot of land to have a garden in your play area. You can make a container garden by filling a wheelbarrow or large pots with rich soil.

**Swings**—If you can set up a swing set, try to include swings designed for different ages. Once infants can sit, you can place them in fully enclosed swings that are high enough off the ground so that they can see what is going on around them. Toddlers and twos can use bucket swings. Swings with a single-strap seat are appropriate for preschool and school-age children.

**Slides**—A number of companies make sturdy slide structures. Locate them on soft cushioning material. If your outdoor area has a hill, you can embed a slide in the ground, thereby making it safe for even very young children. Check a metal slide each time you take children outdoors on a sunny day, to be sure that it is not too hot.

**Platforms and climbers**—Climbers do not need to be higher than 18 inches from the ground, and cushioning material should be underneath and around them. Low, wide steps or a ramp can lead to a platform that is large enough for two or three children at a time. There should be handholds for children to grab when they need to steady themselves. Made of wood or plastic, structures with different levels provide challenges for children of different ages. You can fasten a steering wheel on one level to encourage dramatic play.

**Sandboxes**—You can purchase or make a sandbox out of wood, use a large tractor tire, or fill basins that can be moved around. Purchase sanitized sand and keep it protected from animals.

**Water tubs**—A table, trough, or tubs to hold water will delight children on hot days. Make sure that whatever you use can be emptied easily after each use. Germs collect easily in standing water and become a breeding site for mosquitoes. A hose, by itself or with a sprinkler, is another way to provide water for outdoor play.

**Tires**—Automobile tires can be embedded in the ground to make climbing structures. Children can climb into and out of them and sit for a while. Remove any water that collects in tires so they don't become a breeding site for mosquitoes. (If you poke large holes in the bottoms before placing them in the ground, water will drain.)

**Playhouses, boats, and tunnels**—You can purchase playhouses or construct them with the help of families. An old rowboat, sanded and painted, would be a great addition if you have room. Plastic trash cans with the bottoms cut out make inexpensive tunnels. You can also purchase tunnels of cloth–covered, expandable wire. They can be collapsed for easy storage when not in use.

**Cardboard cartons**—While not permanent structures, the cartons from computers and household appliances can be transformed into tunnels, playhouses, cars, or places for children to be alone for a while. Cut large windows and doors so that you can see the children at all times.

## Providing Outdoor Experiences

In addition to the equipment described above, think about the kinds of experiences children most enjoy outdoors and what materials you can bring outdoors for them. Here are some ideas:

**Digging in sand and mud, and pouring water**—These are enjoyable experiences for children of all ages and ideal to offer outdoors where messiness is not a problem.

Good sand areas are large enough for several children to play without feeling crowded. If possible, locate the sand area close to a water supply, such as an outdoor faucet or water fountain, so children can experiment with both wet and dry sand. If you do not have a nearby source of water, use pails, pitchers, or spray bottles to transport water to the sand area. Offer water play in tubs or wading pools if you do not have running water outside. Remember to empty the water after each use.

Props enhance digging, pouring, constructing, and dramatic play with mud, sand, and water. Chapter 15, "Sand and Water," offers a list of props for children of various ages. Here is a partial list:

- buckets, mixing bowls, pails, plastic containers
- shovels, spoons, and scoops of all sizes
- funnels, strainers, and sifters
- pots, pans, and molds
- measuring spoons and cups
- muffin tins
- plastic pitchers and jugs
- sand or water wheels and pumps
- small wheelbarrows
- plastic figurines of people and animals
- craft sticks
- natural materials such as shells, sticks, leaves, stones
- toy vehicles

**Pulling, pushing, and riding wheeled toys**—These toys are popular once children become mobile and steady in their movements. They use their large-muscle skills to push and pull toys such as shopping carts, baby carriages, lawn mowers, and wagons. They learn to propel themselves forward or backward on riding toys by pushing with their feet, and they eventually learn to pedal and steer a tricycle. Riding toys require a hard surface, and children must wear helmets. Yard sales are a good source of these toys.

You can enhance children's play by adding signs, chalk, road markers, directional arrows, and big orange cones to control traffic. Props can help children imagine that a wheeled toy is an ambulance, a fire truck, or a mail truck and inspire children to create a gas station or car wash.

**Rolling, throwing, bouncing, and catching**—Balls are a favorite toy of all children. Outdoors, you can add the challenge of large balls like beach balls, soccer balls, and basketballs. For preschool and school-age children, who enjoy ball games with simple rules, a basketball hoop provides an added challenge. Tightly sewn bean bags to throw into a basket are another option.

**Collecting, dumping, and filling**—This is a favorite activity of young children, and it is easy to provide the materials they need. Small pails and buckets with handles are perfect for collecting small objects, whether they are natural materials like leaves, seeds, shells, and rocks or they are toys you bring outdoors. Beware of choking hazards.

**Constructing**—Large plastic blocks are a great addition to outdoor play. So are empty boxes and planks that children can build with and walk along. Bales of hay, tires, and plastic pipes with elbows can be used for building projects.

**Gardening**—Children can help you plant and care for a variety of flowers, herbs, and vegetables. Even 2-year-olds can help water the garden, check the plants each day for changes, help with the harvest, and enjoy the results. Preschool and school-age children can help weed the garden and monitor the growth of plants.

---

## Recommended Plants[4]

- Plants that attract butterflies: butterfly bushes, asters, dill, parsley, and hollyhocks
- Plants that provide color, texture, scent and taste: lamb's ears, sage, mint, marigold, and basil
- Vegetables and fruit that are easy to grow: cherry tomatoes, yellow pear tomatoes, peas, string beans, melons, carrots, broccoli, and potatoes

**Observing living things**—Children are fascinated by living things. Notice the excitement of a 2-year-old who spots birds, ants, squirrels, caterpillars, and worms! Bug boxes enable children to collect and observe caterpillars or worms that they are reluctant to hold. Provide magnifying glasses for closer examinations. In many settings, nature provides just about everything you need outdoors. You can also attract living things to your outdoor area. For example, here's what you might do to attract birds to your yard:

- Hang birdfeeders and birdhouses.
- Create a birdbath by turning large flowerpot upside down and putting a large saucer on top for water.
- Grow plants that produce berries and seeds that birds like to eat.
- Put out materials that birds use to build nests, for example, twigs, straw, string, and ribbons.

If you provide pictures and field guides, older preschool and school-age children can identify and learn about the birds that visit. They can read books and use the Internet to find the information they want.

**Caring for pets**—Pets such as rabbits, hamsters, gerbils, and guinea pigs give children the opportunity to care for animals and to be responsible for them. They can also observe growth, other changes, and the habits of animals. Very young children need to be taught how to handle, hold, and pet animals without injuring them.

Cages for should be large enough for a pet to move around without getting hurt, and they must be cleaned frequently. The location of the cage is important, because animals must be protected from weather and other animals if they are left out at night. In some cases, taking pets inside at night is best. Be sure to check with a pet store or vet to be sure you give a pet the right food.

**Playing games**—Children enjoy playing many traditional games outdoors, such as tag, hide-and-seek, "Red Light/Green Light," "Simon Says," hopscotch, and follow the leader. They also love scavenger hunts with hints and simple maps. You can bring out some bubble solution and have children chase bubbles. Provide hula hoops and jump ropes for older preschool and school-age children, and offer a large parachute if possible.

**Creating with art materials**—Bringing art materials outdoors provides a different experience for children. Large colored chalk, brushes and paint, and playdough can all be brought outdoors. The colors look even brighter in sunlight, and children can paint with greater freedom of movement. On a warm day, children might like to try foot and toe painting on butcher paper. (Mixing the paint with liquid soap makes it easier to wash off.) A small outdoor picnic table is the perfect place for children to color with crayons and markers, mold with clay or dough, paste collages, and glue wood.

**Walking in the neighborhood**—Take a look around your neighborhood with children's interests in mind. What interesting places and experiences are within walking distance? Are there stores to visit, a post office where you and the children can mail letters, or a construction site the children can visit regularly to watch a building go up?

Occasionally take a "let's look" walk and have children look for something in particular, such as shapes, shadows, seeds, or leaves. Young children love to collect what they find, so take along containers or bags for their collections. Challenge the older children to take a "let's find out" walk. For example, encourage them to discover

- signs of spring (or fall)
- bird and squirrel nests
- different leaves and seeds
- the kinds of trucks used at a construction site
- how much litter is in the neighborhood
- why shadows change sizes
- what kinds of stores are in the neighborhood

When you return from a walk, invite the older children to draw pictures of what they saw and to dictate stories. Provide props for dramatic play related to the places you visited. Offer books and invite children to use the Internet to learn more.

## Meeting Special Needs

The outdoors can be overwhelming and even frightening for a child who is not sure about how to get around an open space safely. Think about your outdoor space from each child's point of view. For example, a child with a visual disability will need to be oriented to the locations of play structures. Encourage the child to touch the equipment as you describe its features and guide his first attempts to use it. Stay nearby to supervise and teach other children to assist children with visual impairments. For a child with a hearing problem, point out places to be careful, such as where to watch out for tricycles. Remind the child to look carefully in all directions before running across the yard.

Consult with experts and the child's family to learn about adaptations to meet the needs of individual children. Here are some examples of outdoor adaptations:

- Use bucket seats with straps on swings.
- Build ramps over uneven surfaces or inclines for children who use wheelchairs or who have poor balance.
- Place handholds and rails on climbing equipment and structures.
- Offer sand and water play, art, and other activities at a table so children in wheelchairs can participate fully.
- Place straps on the pedals of wheeled toys.

# Caring and Teaching

One of the challenges in taking children of different ages outdoors is managing all of the details. A bit of planning can go a long way, so it is worth the effort. Your enthusiasm for being outdoors, your interest in the discoveries children make and the new skills they develop, and your appreciation of nature will be contagious.

## Managing the Details

Getting a group of children toileted, dressed, and ready to go outside can challenge even the most organized provider, especially when the weather requires extra clothing and boots. Keep in mind that dressing involves many learning opportunities for children. Here are some ways to make getting ready easier:

- Teach children the "family child care flip" for putting on jackets and sweaters. These are the steps of the flip:
  - Place the jacket or sweater on the floor with the inside facing up and the hood or collar at your feet.
  - Put your arms in the sleeves and flip the jacket over your head.
- Encourage the children to put on their own hats, mittens, and scarves as soon as they are interested and able to do so.
- Give the children time to practice self-help skills at other times of the day. For a younger child, start the zipper and let the the child pull it up.
- Encourage older children who know how to tie, button, and zip to help the younger children.

Getting everyone dressed is half the challenge. You can also take steps to make it easier to manage children outdoors.

- Have the equipment you need for transporting infants and toddlers (for example, a double stroller, a backpack, or a baby carrier). Encourage toddlers and twos to walk at least part of the way.
- Use a backpack or attach a sack to the stroller and keep it packed with whatever you need for outdoor time. For example, include snack crackers, tissues, baby wipes, diapers, plastic bags, paper towels, spare clothes, something to sit on, a first-aid kit, and a book to read to the children. Check the supplies each night so you only have to add something for the children to drink in order to be ready the next day.
- Ask children to help carry things outside or to the park. Preschoolers and school-age children can wear backpacks with a few items in each.
- Set some basic, simple rules for the older children to follow when all of you go for a walk. For example, have children hold hands or hold onto the stroller. Give simple directions, for example, "You may walk to the corner, but stop at the tree."

- Coordinate with another provider for neighborhood walks or extended mornings at the park. Although you will have to watch more children, joint adult supervision will give both of you more flexibility in planning for the children. You will also enjoy the adult company.

- Encourage children's independence outdoors. Show them where outdoor equipment is stored so they can help carry and return things.

## Encouraging Children to Explore Safely

Outdoor time can be a little intimidating for some children, especially when you take them to a new playground. If they do not know what to do in large open spaces and on challenging play structures, they will need your help and encouragement. Some children want to feel your hand on their waists as they climb to the top of the slide or to have you stand at the bottom to catch them. Others just want to know that you are nearby. You might ask, "How can I help you feel safe?" Climbing up a single rung of the jungle gym may be as big an accomplishment for one child as climbing to the top is for another child.

Some children ask for constant acknowledgment, insisting, "Look at me!" or "Watch what I can do!" As much as possible, let children experience a sense of their own competence without relying on your praise. You might try telling a child, "Wow! You climbed to the top of the slide all by yourself. How does that make you feel?" or "I bet you're pretty proud of yourself right now."

You must always intervene when children are not safe. In unsafe situations, give clear, specific directions. Simply calling out a child's name if she is walking too close to the swings may not have much of an effect. She might stand still and look at you, but she will not necessarily move away. She will be likely to move if you say, "Keisha, move back! You are too close to the swings." Then you can show her where she can walk safely.

## Appreciating the Natural Environment

One of the greatest benefits of taking children outdoors is the opportunity to nurture their appreciation of the natural environment. You don't have to be a naturalist to support children's delight with the world and their desire to discover what is around them. Even urban environments offer elements of nature to study and enjoy.

More than ever before, nurturing an appreciation for nature is important. Many children have never experienced the joy of tramping through the woods, rolling down a grassy hill, looking for life in a pond, digging in mud, or turning rocks over to find insects. If we want children to grow up to care about preserving the environment, we have to start early to foster a love for it.

You can be a model for children by demonstrating your own excitement and curiosity about the natural world. Focus on having fun with children when you go outdoors and share your enthusiasm for their discoveries.

Suppose, for example, that several children uncover some bugs outdoors and are fascinated by watching them. By showing an interest and asking open-ended questions, you can encourage children to observe, predict, and draw conclusions. These are process skills that scientists use.

Here are examples of what you might say:

"What did you find? Tell me what you see."

"How are they different from one another?"

"What do you think they are doing?"

"How do they move?"

"What do you think they like to eat?"

"How can we find out more about them?"

The outdoor environment is full of surprises for those who use all of their senses to explore what is all around. You never know what children might find when they pay attention to it.

## Responding to Each Child

What children do and how they experience the outdoors vary according to their age, skills, and interests. Your careful supervision and responsiveness support positive experiences for each child.

**Infants** need to be in a protected area where they can see everything that is going on and be safe from children who are running and jumping. They want to crawl, cruise, and climb as they become more mobile, so you have to provide a safe area for them to explore. They also enjoy playing with water, pushing wheeled toys, and dumping and filling containers.

| Observe | Reflect | Respond |
| --- | --- | --- |
| Jeremy is sitting on a blanket in the backyard, watching the older children play with a ball. He rocks back and forth excitedly when it rolls nearby, gets on his hands and knees, and crawls toward the ball. Nathan gets to it first, and Jeremy starts to cry. He calms down when you show him another ball and hand it to him. | Jeremy is able to sit by himself and crawl to where he wants to be. *(Objective 4. Demonstrates traveling skills)*<br><br>He knows what he wants and responds to redirection when he gets upset *(Objective 1, Regulates own emotions and behaviors)* | Talk with Jeremy about what is happening: "You saw Jorge and Nathan playing with a ball. You want one, too. We have lots of balls, so you can play with a ball like the other children."<br><br>Suggest a way to use the ball: "Let me show you how to roll the ball. Now roll it to me. Then I'll roll it right back to you!" |

**Toddlers and twos** are usually enthusiastic about going outdoors. Their developing gross and fine motor skills give them more control as they explore. Close supervision is a must. Toddlers and twos can move quickly and climb, slide, and jump in a flash. Stay alert and try to anticipate what children will do so you can be prepared to step in when needed.

| Observe | Reflect | Respond |
| --- | --- | --- |
| Tamika walks around the park, holding your hand. She points to some fallen leaves and asks, "Dat?" Bending down, she picks one up and hands it to you. Then she picks up another.<br><br>When Jorge comes by, she hands him a leaf. Jorge says, "Gracias, Tamika", throws the leaf in the air, and watches it fall. Tamika picks up another leaf and throws it up in the air, laughing. | Tamika has noticed the leaves and wants to share her discovery with us. *(Objective 2, Establishes and sustains positive relationships)*<br><br>She is using word-like sounds to communicate. *(Objective 9, Uses spoken language to express thoughts and needs)*<br><br>Tamika uses both small and large muscles when she picks up and tosses leaves. *(Objective 6, Demonstrates gross motor manipulative skills; Objective 7, Demonstrates fine motor strength and coordination)* | To promote her language development, talk about what Tamika is doing: "Tamika, you found some leaves, and you want to share them with Jorge and me."<br><br>Support her interest in imitating what Jorge does: "Jorge threw his leaf in the air and watched it fall. Then you threw the leaf up, too."<br><br>Encourage her interest in playing with others: "There are so many leaves on the ground! Let's see how many you two can throw in the air. Wow, it's raining leaves!" |

**Preschool and school-age children** have many ideas about what to do outdoors, and they head outside with a plan: to ride a tricycle, play ball, paint the fence with water, shoot baskets, or try to catch a butterfly. They are likely to make requests about what materials to bring outside or where to walk. As always, your attention to their interests enhances opportunities for learning.

| Observe | Reflect | Respond |
|---|---|---|
| "Oh," exclaims Rosa, pointing to a caterpillar in the garden. She lifts the caterpillar gently from a leaf and examines it. The other children gather around.<br><br>"Yuk," exclaims Jorge, "I no like worms."<br><br>Tyrone comes to see and says, "That's a caterpillar, and it likes tomato plants. It's a tomato caterpillar, I bet." | Rosa has noticed something interesting outdoors and is curious about it. *(Objective 11, Demonstrates positive approaches to learning)*<br><br>Tyrone is also interested in the caterpillar and seems to want to identify it. | Ask questions: "Do you think that caterpillar eats the tomato plants? Did you actually see it eating the leaves? How can we find out for sure?"<br><br>Help the children put the caterpillar carefully in a jar so they can observe it for a while. Offer a book about caterpillars or suggest looking on the Internet to find out what kind it is. |

## Engaging Children of All Ages Outdoors

Outdoor time can be really relaxed and fun. Children of all ages can interact with each other outdoors, just as they do indoors. However, outdoor time can also present some challenges. You must balance the children's interests with the need to supervise a group of children of varying ages and different strengths and needs.

It's a lovely afternoon, so there is no need to put on hats and coats before you head to the backyard with your group. Jeremy (8 months) is tucked into your frontpack, where you think he'll be falling asleep as you jostle him gently by moving. Nathan (3 years), Rosa (4 years), and Keisha (4 ½ years) have been gardening, so you give them child-sized shovels to continue digging where they stopped yesterday. Tamika (19 months) joins the gardening crew, but she's not interested in digging. No, Tamika appears to be having a tasty snack of dirt!

After a quick swipe at Tamika's face with a damp wipe, you manage to redirect her to a blanket in a shady spot in the yard where she can look at books. You're about to stroll

back to the gardening area when Jeremy wakes up. He wants his bottle, and he wants it now! You move your outdoor glider near the garden, so you can feed Jeremy while you chat with the gardeners and watch Tamika, who is on the blanket.

Soon the gardeners are ready for a break from digging. They join Tamika on the blanket, talking about their gardening project. Keisha wonders, "How will we know what vegetables we planted?" Tyrone (8 years), the school-age expert, volunteers to help the preschool children make signs for the garden. He walks to the picnic table and begins to make signs with the paper, crayons, and scissors that are on the table.

Bottle finished, you put Jeremy in his stroller and wheel him around as all of the children join you in a game of tag before trooping indoors for a refreshing afternoon snack.

Keep these points about outdoor time in mind:

- Allow children to have different play experiences outdoors.

- Ask children questions that will extend their play, and join their play when doing so is appropriate. Sometimes that means holding a conversation while supervising or taking care of other children.

- Remember that activities such as reading or looking at books, dramatic play, art, and playing with toys can take place outdoors as well as indoors. Sometimes encourage children to be quiet and relaxed outdoors. This can be a time for being peaceful as well as for rough-and-tumble, large-muscle play.

- Schedule outdoor play sensibly, considering the weather and the length of time necessary for whatever outdoor activities you are planning.

- Plan for outdoor time just as you do for indoor time, but remember to be flexible and follow the children's lead.

Make outdoor time a part of everyday life in your program. You will enjoy the time you spend with the children outside, and the benefits for the children will last a lifetime.

# Partnering With Families

You can build your partnerships with families by using and sending home *LearningGames*® activities and by sharing the letter to families about going outdoors.

## *LearningGames*® for Outdoor Play

### Birth–12 months

**Game 25, "Showing What Comes Next"**

Encourage the family to play this game with their baby when they go outdoors. Each time they get ready to go outdoors, they can show the baby a related object, such as a jacket or hat, and describe it. The baby will begin to make sense of the world by associating objects with actions and words, and he or she will begin to understand what happens next. Model how you do this in your program. At the end of the day you can say something like this: "Here's your hat. It's time to go home with Daddy."

### 12–24 months

**Game 60, "Exploring Outdoors"**

Help families think about what they can do outdoors with their babies. Babies love to explore the world outdoors, to see, feel, smell, and sometimes even taste what they find. They can examine leaves, flowers, sticks, sand, and rocks, and they learn new words as they listen to their families describe what they are seeing and touching. As toddlers walk around outside your home, talk about the interesting things they look at and touch.

24–36 months

### Game 90, "A Fun Path"

This *LearningGames* activity helps children strengthen their physical skills and understand the positions of their bodies in space. Encourage families to describe their children's actions and to use positional words, such as *in, out, around, under,* and *over,* as their child moves through the obstacle course they make together. Show parents how you use ordinary materials to create a fun path for the children.

36–48 months

### Game 117, "Ride a Trike"

Remind families of what children do as they ride trikes: stop, start, pedal, steer, and so on. They are learning a new way to move through space. As they build their physical skills, they can also learn lots of new words: *slow, fast, path, wheels, handlebars, seat, pedal,* and *helmet* are just a few. Let families know which words you are using to support the skills children are learning as they ride tricycles.

48–60 months

### Game 183, "Three-Corner Catch"

This game of toss and catch involves three people, so the child practices taking turns as she practices the physical skills of throwing and catching. Adding a friend or two makes the game even more fun. This game can change as the children become more skilled at throwing and catching. Explain to families that you also play this game with their children and that you keep it interesting and fun by adding more players, using balls of various sizes, or increasing the distance between children.

---

[1] National Association for Family Child Care. (2005). *Quality standards for NAFCC accreditation* (4th ed.). [Electronic version]. Retrieved February 8, 2009, from http://www.nafcc.org/accreditation/accredstandards.asp

[2] American Academy of Pediatrics, American Public Health Association, and National Resource Center for Health and Safety in Child Care and Early Education. (2002). *Caring for our children: National health and safety standards:Guidelines for out-of-home child care programs* (2nd ed.). Elk Grove Village, IL: AAP and Washington, DC: APHA. Also available at http://nrckids.org.

[3] From *Caring for our children: National health and safety standards: Guidelines for out-of-home child care programs* (2nd ed.) (p. 263), by American Academy of Pediatrics, American Public Health Association, and National Resource Center for Health and Safety in Child Care and Early Education, 2002, Elk Grove Village, IL: AAP and Washington, DC: APHA. Copyright 2002 by AAP, APHA, and NRCHSCC. Reprinted with permission.

[4] Torquati, J., & Barber, J. (2005). Dancing with trees: Infants and toddlers in the garden. *Young Children, 60*(3), 43.

# A Letter to Families About Going Outdoors

Dear Families,

I take children outdoors every day, giving them an entirely different environment to explore. Outdoors they can stretch, breathe fresh air, take in the sunshine (or the rain or snow), and enjoy the freedom of open space. They can run, jump, swing, climb, and use their large and small muscles. They marvel at the creatures they find, watch trees move in the wind, and collect seeds and leaves. I want to give the children opportunities to appreciate nature and wonder about their discoveries.

Unless the weather is extreme, we go outdoors several times a day. Sometimes we go for a neighborhood walk and talk about everything we see: a construction project, squirrels, perhaps someone delivering a package. We look for things to collect outdoors, such as leaves, seeds, and dandelions. We talk about weather changes and what animals do. During our time outdoors, the children can move freely and develop their large-muscle skills. Physical exercise and fresh air are essential to your child's health and well-being.

Here are some activities to try next time you go outdoors with your child. You probably do some of them already. Perhaps others are new ideas.

**Enjoy nature.** Talk about the breeze touching your child's cheeks. Roll down a grassy hill together. Plant a garden in your yard, in a window box, or in a wheelbarrow that you can move as the sun moves. Take a bucket so your child can collect things such as feathers and leaves. Be sure that the items do not present a choking hazard.

**Take a texture walk.** Call your child's attention to natural materials and describe them. For example, you might point out *soft* sand, *rough* pinecones, and a *smooth* rock.

**Invent games.** Create a balancing path by laying a piece of rope on the ground to walk along. Play a game of catch. Set up a bowling game in which your child tries to knock down empty food boxes by rolling a beach ball.

**Visit public playgrounds.** Look for playgrounds with equipment appropriate for your child's age and skills. Playgrounds offer wonderful opportunities for children to test their developing skills and play with other children.

**Encourage your school-age child to participate in outdoor activities.** Try to arrange for your child to participate in sports. Take nature walks together and spend as much time as possible outdoors with your child.

Together, we can promote your child's health and well-being by providing outdoor time every day.

Sincerely,

# Appendix

# Selecting Developmentally Appropriate Software

☐ The content and approach are age-appropriate.

☐ The program makes use of the child's interest, not external rewards.

☐ The program is paced so children do not have to wait a long time for the program to load or for graphics or feedback to appear.

☐ The child can use and adjust controls independently, without adult assistance.

☐ The program offers choices that child can control, including the level of difficulty.

☐ The program is open-ended and engages children in exploration and problem-solving activities.

☐ The child can set the pace for movement through the program and exit at any time.

☐ The instructions are clear and simple, and nonreaders can figure out what to do.

☐ Feedback uses meaningful graphics and sound, and it is individualized.

☐ The program appeals to a variety of learning styles.

☐ Adults can track the child's use of the program.

☐ The content and feedback are bias-free and violence-free.

☐ The program is accessible to all children, including those who are dual-language learners and those with disabilities.

☐ The program offers good value for the cost.

☐ The program is fun!

# LearningGames® and Objectives for Development and Learning: Birth to Age 6

| *LearningGames* Activity | Objectives |
|---|---|
| 4, "Soothing Your Baby" | 1. Regulates own emotions and behaviors<br>9. Uses spoken language to express thoughts and needs |
| 12, "Watching a Toy Go Out of Sight" | 11. Demonstrates positive approaches to learning.<br>12. Remembers and connects experiences |
| 14, "Show Feelings" | 2. Establishes and sustains positive relationships<br>8. Listens to and understands increasingly complex language |
| 16, "Ride a Horsie" | 8. Listens to and understands increasingly complex language<br>12. Remembers and connects experiences<br>35. Explores dance and movement concepts |
| 19, "Reading Pictures and Books" | 8. Listens to and understands increasingly complex language<br>17. Demonstrates knowledge of print and its uses<br>18. Comprehends and responds to books and other texts |
| 24, "Dropping Objects" | 7. Demonstrates fine motor strength and coordination<br>9. Uses spoken language to express thoughts, feelings, and needs<br>11. Demonstrates positive approaches to learning |
| 25, "Showing What Comes Next" | 12. Remembers and connects experiences |

| *LearningGames* Activity | Objectives |
|---|---|
| 26, "Imitating Actions" | 2. Establishes and sustains positive relationships |
| | 11. Demonstrates positive approaches to learning |
| | 34. Explores musical concepts and expression |
| 29, "Hi and Bye-Bye" | 10. Uses appropriate conversational and other communication skills |
| 31, "First Crayons" | 7. Demonstrates fine motor strength and coordination |
| | 19. Demonstrates emergent writing skills |
| 32, "Things to Taste" | 9. Uses spoken language to express thoughts and needs |
| 34, "Making Useful Choices" | 8. Listens to and understands increasingly complex language |
| | 11. Demonstrates positive approaches to learning |
| | 13. Classifies and sorts |
| 37. "Animal Sounds" | 15. Demonstrates phonological awareness |
| | 38. Comprehends and responds to books and other texts |
| 41, "Learning to Predict" | 12. Remembers and connects experiences |
| | 13. Classifies and sorts |
| 42, "Making Undressing Easy" | 7. Demonstrates fine motor strength and coordination |
| 45, "Water Play" | 7. Demonstrates fine motor strength and coordination |
| | 9. Uses spoken language to express thoughts and needs |

| *LearningGames* Activity | Objectives |
|---|---|
| 46, "Hide and Seek" | 11. Demonstrates positive approaches to learning<br><br>4. Demonstrates traveling skills |
| 49, "Sing Together" | 15. Demonstrates phonological awareness<br><br>34. Explores musical concepts and expression |
| 50, "Nesting Objects" | 7. Demonstrates fine motor strength and coordination<br><br>21. Explores and describes shapes and spatial relationships<br><br>22. Compares and measures |
| 53, "Build Together" | 11. Demonstrates positive approaches to learning<br><br>23. Demonstrates knowledge of patterns |
| 56, "Expressing Needs" | 9. Uses spoken language to express thoughts and needs |
| 59, "Beginning to Share" | 2. Establishes and sustains positive relationships |
| 60, "Exploring Outdoors" | 11. Demonstrates positive approaches to learning<br><br>8. Listens to and understands increasingly complex language |
| 62, "Painting With Water" | 1. Regulates own emotions and behavior<br><br>7. Demonstrates fine motor strength and coordination<br><br>33. Explores the visual arts |
| 64, "Trying New Motions" | 4. Demonstrates traveling skills<br><br>5. Demonstrates balancing skills<br><br>8. Listens to and understands increasingly complex language<br><br>11. Demonstrates positive approaches to learning.<br><br>35. Explores dance and movement concepts |

| *LearningGames* Activity | Objectives |
|---|---|
| 67, "See, Show, Say" | 8. Listens to and understands increasingly complex language |
| | 18. Comprehends and responds to books and other texts |
| 69, "Create a Face" | 1. Regulates own emotions and behaviors. |
| 71, "Dress-Up Play" | 14. Uses symbols and images to represent something not present |
| | 29. Demonstrates knowledge about self |
| 72, "Tell Me in a Mirror" | 1. Regulates own emotions and behaviors. |
| | 7. Demonstrates fine motor strength and coordination |
| | 8. Listens to and understands increasingly complex language |
| | 14. Uses symbols and images to represent something not present |
| 73, "See It a New Way" | 10. Uses appropriate conversational and other communication skills |
| | 11. Demonstrates positive approaches to learning |
| | 12. Remembers and connects experiences |
| | 13. Classifies and sorts |
| 75, "Sharing Nursery Rhymes" | 8. Listens to and understands increasingly complex language |
| | 15. Demonstrates phonological awareness |
| | 34. Explores musical concepts and expression |
| 77, "Color Sorting" | 8. Listens to and understands increasingly complex language |
| | 13. Classifies and sorts |
| 78, "Building Blocks" | 11. Demonstrates positive approaches to learning |
| | 20. Uses number concepts and operations |

| *LearningGames* Activity | Objectives |
|---|---|
| 90, "A Fun Path" | 4. Demonstrates traveling skills |
| | 5. Demonstrates balancing skills |
| | 8. Listens to and understands increasingly complex language |
| 91, "Words for Time" | 8. Listens to and understands increasingly complex language |
| | 12. Remembers and connects experiences |
| | 18. Comprehends and responds to books and other texts |
| | 29. Demonstrates knowledge about self |
| 95, "Cut and Paste" | 7. Demonstrates fine motor strength and coordination |
| 96, "Help Him Help Himself" | 7. Demonstrates fine motor strength and coordination |
| 98, "Run and Walk Together" | 4. Demonstrates traveling skills |
| | 8. Listens to and understands increasingly complex language |
| | 35. Explores dance and movement concepts |
| 99, "Tell Family Stories" | 14. Uses symbols and images to represent something not present |
| 100, "See Something That Is…" | 11. Demonstrates positive approaches to learning |
| | 13. Classifies and sorts |
| 101, "Soap Curls" | 1. Regulates own emotions and behavior |
| | 7. Demonstrates fine motor strength and coordination |
| 106, "Seeing Feelings" | 2. Establishes and sustains positive relationships |

| *LearningGames* Activity | Objectives |
|---|---|
| 108, "Planting Together" | 3. Participates cooperatively and constructively in group situations |
| | 11. Demonstrates positive approaches to learning |
| | 25. Demonstrates knowledge of the characteristics of living things |
| 111, "Compare Two Amounts" | 22. Compares and measures |
| 115, "Stories With Three" | 20. Uses number concepts and operations |
| 117, "Ride a Trike" | 4. Demonstrates traveling skills |
| | 10. Uses appropriate conversational and other communication skills |
| 118, "Button and Zip" | 7. Demonstrates fine motor strength and coordination |
| 119, "Two-Step Directions" | 1. Regulates own emotions and behavior. |
| | 8. Listens to and understands increasingly complex language |
| 121, "See and Show" | 10. Uses appropriate conversational and other communication skills |
| | 12. Remembers and connects experiences |
| 122, "Searching for Sounds" | 11. Demonstrates positive approaches to learning |
| | 12. Remembers and connects experiences |
| | 34. Explores musical concepts and expression |
| 123, "Painting With My Hands" | 7. Demonstrates fine motor strength and coordination |
| | 33. Explores the visual arts |
| 130, "Matching Among Similar Pictures" | 13. Classifies and sorts |
| | 17. Demonstrates knowledge of print and its uses |
| | 18. Comprehends and responds to books and other texts |
| | 33. Explores the visual arts |

| _LearningGames_ Activity | Objectives |
|---|---|
| 133, "Packing My Own Picnic" | 11. Demonstrates positive approaches to learning |
| | 12. Remembers and connects experiences |
| 147, "Props for Pretending" | 13. Classifies and sorts |
| | 14. Uses symbols and images to represent something not present |
| 154, "Inspect and Collect" | 11. Demonstrates positive approaches to learning |
| | 13. Classifies and sorts |
| | 24. Uses scientific inquiry skills |
| | 26. Demonstrates knowledge of the physical properties of objects and materials |
| 157, "Fork Foods" | 7. Demonstrates fine motor strength and coordination |
| | 11. Classifies and sorts |
| | 9. Uses spoken language to express thoughts and needs |
| 158, "Syllable Jump" | 4. Demonstrates traveling skills |
| | 7. Demonstrates fine motor strength and coordination |
| | 15. Demonstrates phonological awareness |
| | 35. Explores dance and movement concepts |
| 159, "When, How, Why" | 9. Uses spoken language to express thoughts and needs |
| | 12. Remembers and connects experiences |
| 160, "Move Up Five" | 20. Uses number concepts and operations |
| 168, "Build a Person" | 7. Demonstrates fine motor strength and coordination |
| | 11. Demonstrates positive approaches to learning |

| *LearningGames* Activity | Objectives |
|---|---|
| 171, "Add to the Tale" | 7. Demonstrates fine motor strength and coordination<br>31. Comprehends and responds to books and other texts |
| 174, "Which Is Best?" | 11. Demonstrates positive approaches to learning |
| 177, "Today I Can" | 11. Demonstrates positive approaches to learning |
| 179, "Mailing a Letter" | 7. Demonstrates fine motor strength and coordination<br>30. Shows basic understanding of people and how they live |
| 183, "Three Corner Catch" | 2. Establishes and sustains positive relationships<br>5. Participates cooperatively and constructively in group situations<br>6. Demonstrates gross motor manipulative skills<br>9. Uses spoken language to express thoughts and needs |
| 184, "I'd Like to Help" | 9. Uses spoken language to express thoughts and needs<br>2. Establishes and sustains positive relationships |
| 189, "Let's Imagine" | 9. Uses spoken language to express thoughts and needs<br>11. Demonstrates positive approaches to learning<br>18. Comprehends and responds to books and other texts |
| 190, "Wondering What Caused It" | 11. Demonstrates positive approaches to learning<br>12. Remembers and connects experiences<br>24. Uses scientific inquiry skills |

# Index

# Order Form
Please type or print clearly.

**Teaching**Strategies™

## Ship to:

ORGANIZATION

ADDRESS

| CITY | STATE | ZIP |
| --- | --- | --- |
| PHONE | FAX | |

E-MAIL

## Bill to:

ORGANIZATION

ADDRESS

| CITY | STATE | ZIP |
| --- | --- | --- |
| PHONE | FAX | |

E-MAIL

YOUR TEACHING STRATEGIES CUSTOMER NUMBER: (If known)

## Order:

| ITEM # | QTY | DESCRIPTION | UNIT PRICE | TOTAL |
| --- | --- | --- | --- | --- |
| | | | $ | $ |
| | | | $ | $ |
| | | | $ | $ |
| | | | $ | $ |
| | | | $ | $ |
| | | | $ | $ |
| | | | $ | $ |
| | | | $ | $ |

Please call for information on quantity discounts.

| | |
| --- | --- |
| SUBTOTAL | $ |
| SALES TAX  CA, IL, MD, NC: Add appropriate sales tax. | $ |
| SHIPPING  **United States:** Orders up to $60.00—$5.00; Orders over $60.00—12% of total. **International/U.S. Territories:** $20.00 (first book) + $10.00 for each additional book. **Rush Delivery:** Call for shipping charges. **Method:** ❏ 2-day  ❏ 3-day  ❏ Next-day  ❏ International | $ |
| TOTAL | $ |

## Method of payment:

All orders must be accompanied by payment, P.O. number, or credit card information. Customers with an established credit history are welcome to use P.O. numbers. **First-time customers must enclose pre-payment with order.**

❏ Check (payable to Teaching Strategies)     ❏ Money order

❏ Purchase order (must include copy of P.O. )     ❏ Visa          ❏ MasterCard

❏ American Express     ❏ Discover

CREDIT CARD OR PURCHASE ORDER NUMBER          EXPIRATION DATE

SIGNATURE OF CARD HOLDER

❏ Yes, I would like to receive occasional e-mail notifications about new Teaching Strategies products and special offers. I understand that Teaching Strategies will not share or sell my e-mail address with any other individual, company, or organization.

**Guarantee:** Teaching Strategies guarantees your complete satisfaction. If you are not happy with your order, simply return the item(s) in sellable condition within 30 days for a full refund, excluding shipping and handling fees. However, all video/DVD and software sales are final. Teaching Strategies is not responsible for returned items that are lost or misdirected. Prices subject to change without notice.

# Thank you for your order.

# 4 Ways to Order

**Order online**
TeachingStrategies.com

**Order by phone**
800-637-3652
Washington, DC area
301-634-0818
8:30 a.m.–7:00 p.m.
Eastern Time, M–F

**Order by fax**
301-634-0826
24 hours a day

**Order by mail**
Teaching Strategies, Inc.
P.O. Box 42243
Washington, DC 20015